What People Are Sa

Forward

"Change is inevitable. Adaptation is needed to stay alive and to thrive. But most change is neither adaptive nor exciting. Elizabeth Moran steps into this abyss with one of the most enlightening, compassionate, and yet realistic discussions of how to deal with, lead, and inspire change in organizations. She sparks possibilities and hope into these ever-present processes, like a bolt of lightning brought characters in a movie into the future."
Richard Boyatzis, PhD, Distinguished University Professor, Case Western Reserve University, coauthor of the international best seller *Primal Leadership* and the recent *Helping People Change*

"Let's face it. Change is hard, especially when it is thrust upon you. That's why most change initiatives fail to meet their objectives and create significant stress and frustration in leaders and teams. Elizabeth Moran's *Forward* takes these leaders through a compassionate step-by-step approach to first align themselves and then their teams to enable change to flow smoothly."
Henna Inam, CEO of Transformational Leadership Inc. and author of *Wired for Authenticity*

"One of the biggest barriers to change (and learning and growth and, and, and) isn't that great change only happens to some people. It's that most people don't manage it. In increasingly messy times, having a voice like Elizabeth Moran's to guide you through the process not like a stuffy consultant but like a street-smart friend could be the difference between thriving in times of change and devolving into a hot mess. Buy this book."
Mike Rognlien, founder of Multiple Hats Management and author of *This Is Now Your Company: A Culture Carrier's Manifesto*

"Elizabeth offers a refreshing, simple approach to navigating the complexities of leading change, offering a much-needed tool for every leader who feels overwhelmed by the volume and unpredictability of organizational change."
Kevin Kruse, bestselling author of *Great Leaders Have No Rules* and *15 Secrets Successful People Know About Time Management*

Elizabeth provides a must-have guide for leaders to move through common barriers to change, especially how to reduce anxiety and cut through the clutter that causes confusion, helping everyone align and move more confidently into the unknown. While there are many books on the subject, Elizabeth's approach and insights are profound, yet practical, setting the approach apart and in a class of its own. I highly recommend this book!"
Dr. Srini Pillay, author of *Your Brain and Business* and *Tinker, Dabble, Doodle, Try*

Forward will give you time-saving and anxiety-reducing guidance at any stage of a tough change. You'll venture into the unknown with a skilled and trusted coach who understands what it takes to inspire a team to action."
Mark Thompson, New York Times bestselling author of *Success Built to Last* and *Now...Build a Great Business!*

Forward

Leading Your Team Through Change

Forward

Leading Your Team Through Change

Elizabeth Moran

Winchester, UK
Washington, USA

JOHN HUNT PUBLISHING

First published by Business Books, 2023
Business Books is an imprint of John Hunt Publishing Ltd., No. 3 East St., Alresford, Hampshire SO24 9EE, UK
office@jhpbooks.com
www.johnhuntpublishing.com
www.johnhuntpublishing.com/business-books

For distributor details and how to order please visit the 'Ordering' section on our website.

ISBN: 978 1 78279 289 5
978 1 78279 291 8 (ebook)
Library of Congress Control Number: 2021951517

A CIP catalogue record for this book is available from the British Library.

Design: Matthew Greenfield

UK: Printed and bound by CPI Group (UK) Ltd, Croydon, CR0 4YY
Printed in North America by CPI GPS partners

Contents

For Sydney Sutherland,
kindness always through transformation

Acknowledgments

Huge and heartfelt thanks to the friends who helped bring this book to life: Sandy Thomas, Jill Altana, Doug Politi, Mary Azzolini, Doreen Coles, Tim Kopko, Dan Raimondi, Melanie Shook, Cathy Rogers, Greg McCaffery, Rob Brodo, David Foskett, Diana Yarbrough, Vipul Nagrath, Charlotte Jordan Saulny, Jay Caldwell, and Jane Wesman.

Love and blessings to my family and friends who help bring me to life: Ashley du Pont, Kathleen Matschullat, Mary Fahl, Tracy Rosensteel, Evers Whyte, Nick Victor, Jeff Lally, Andy Barker, Nora Infante, Michael Di Vihil, Lyne Desormeaux, Cristiano Tortoioli, Kevyn Wynn, Paula Frank, Laurel Donnellan, Grace Parra, Anne Symon, and Lynne Fuller.

Special thanks to my brilliant and humorous editor, Beth Jusino, who kept me joking on the path more often than pulling my hair out. Also to Kathy Burge for bringing her amazing, meticulous eye to this work. Thanks also to the team at John Hunt Publishing, for seeing the need for this work and giving me the chance to make it real.

And finally, to all you brave and passionate leaders who have been generous with your time and dedicated to your growth—I am honored to be part of your team!

PART I

Practical Change Leadership

Leading human beings in a direction they didn't decide to go is hard, which is why I wrote this book. I am a self-described "change nerd," a title earned after 20 plus years of using my skills to celebrate successes and slog through challenges alongside colleagues and clients trying to transform their organizations in big and small ways. I love this stuff, both because of and in spite of the complexities and frustrations that human beings bring to making changes.

Meeting with leaders and teams one-on-one is great, but as the pace of change in our consolidated, digitized world speeds up, I needed another tool, this one in a format that leaders from all fields, leading teams of all sizes, could easily use during their own periods of change.

To my surprise, this book didn't exist. I could find lots of 300-page resources about the theories and strategies of leading large-scale organizational change (many of which are very good), but seriously, who has the time to sort through all that information for the bits you need most as a team leader? And there were plenty of short articles full of bullet-point lists telling me what to do, but there wasn't enough information about how to do it. The busy people leaders I know—the ones most often called on to implement changes made by others in their organization—need practical tools, conversation guides, and directions to quickly refer back to when they are going through periods of stress and change.

That's what you'll find here. When change is coming from above or externally, and you need to get it done, this guide is here to help you keep change leadership simple and effective. Just to be clear, I use the terms *change leadership* and *change management* interchangeably. For your own purposes, choose whichever synonym you like. This is your playbook of beginning-to-end steps, practical conversation guides, tested actions, and perspective-changing questions. While these pages will not hit on everything unique to your particular situation, we'll explore the most common challenges that I and my clients have worked through.

As you read this book, recall changes you led in the past, or one you need to lead through now, to make what's written come alive for you. You may come across a suggestion or idea that resonates with you because you took that action and had success. Great, you can take this practice forward as you lead your next change. You may also find your past or current change challenges outlined in a story or example shared here. Also great! You can prioritize the suggested action or guidance to help you have more success right now. I invite you to read straight through, skip to chapters that are most relevant, or jump to the back, where I've summarized the whole process in the Forward Change Leadership Tool to help you quickly implement the steps, without a lot of extra reading or detail. Engage with this book in whatever way is most helpful for you. I am excited to give you an inside look at what I have learned and used along the way that has worked!

Chapter 1

Leading Change Is Hard

Your boss pulls you aside and tells you the company is making a change in the product development plan...again. It means they need to release the update your team's been working on 2 months sooner than planned.

"I know this is tough," she says, "but you always get it done...just tell the team."

"Okay," you say, because you know that's what you're supposed to say but also because you *can* see the benefits of a faster release for the clients and the company. You also know that the change is inevitable, and the team will get it done. But it's not going to be easy. Communicating this change *and* getting your team to buy in requires more than just a quick email. The truth is, you're dreading the moment when you have to tell them. You can already imagine how they'll respond, given all the items already on the product backlog and the many other changes that have already been pushed down from above.

"How do they expect us to get this done in time?"

"We're already down a couple of people and working long hours!"

"This is just another decision made by out-of-touch executives who don't understand what it will mean to the rest of us!"

That's what they'll say to your face. It'll be worse when you're not in the room.

So how do you do this? How do you lead your team through this change?

If you're reading this book, chances are you manage people. Whether you've been in a leadership role for a long time or are brand-new to your job, let me state something that you've probably already figured out: change can be hard. This is especially true when you aren't the one to initiate the change. Remember the time your favorite coffee place changed their breakfast blend, and you winced when you tasted the new, "improved" brew? Or when your doctor's office moved to a different part of town, and how irritated you felt every time it took an extra 25 minutes to get to your appointment? Or, more recently, when the global shutdown upended almost everything, and you got hit with a lot of changes all at once? While these range in level of severity, there's one thing they have in common: when change happens to you without your input or agreement, it doesn't feel so great.

Here are some examples of tough changes at work that have happened to me, other leaders, and maybe to you, as well:

- You have to downsize your department and exit people who are really good.
- Your much-loved and supportive boss leaves and is replaced by someone you're not sure will be as supportive or, worse, someone you don't like so much.
- You're ready to launch a process or product when a new "sponsor" takes over and wants to make changes, upending the work you and your team have already done.
- You are told to implement a change you believe is a bad idea.
- Your organization is part of a merger or acquisition that affects everything about your job.

And now it's up to you to guide others through changes that neither you nor they initiated or control, which can feel pretty messy and overwhelming.

A mentor once asked me, "Elizabeth, when is making a change a good idea?" In the middle of overthinking my response, he answered his own question. "When it's your idea!" A light bulb went on for me at that moment.

Your team is made up of humans who are likely to resist change when it's not *their* idea, especially if it's not completely clear how or if the change will be good for them. It's how we're hardwired mentally and emotionally to survive. It's also part of why leading people through periods of change is one of the hardest parts of your job.

I'm one of those people who doesn't mind change. I often need to shake things up when I get too comfortable. I like to think it's because I want to make something better, but sometimes, if I'm really honest, it's because I'm bored. Gift? Curse? Both, actually, depending on the context. Having said that, I'm human and prefer making a change that's *my* idea and decision, and not the other way around.

You Can't Change People

Here's the first thing I want you to know: *your job is not to make people change*. In fact, changing a person is impossible.

Intellectually, you probably already know this. I certainly do, and yet, even after years of therapy, I still find myself trying to change other people, especially when conflict or resistance emerges. Many leaders feel pressure to *make* their team members decide to change. Unfortunately, that doesn't work. People have to decide on their own whether to get on board or to resist. We'll talk about this, and your role in their decision, more in the following chapters.

But the boss still wants that new product to launch, or that new process implemented, so the leader, feeling pressed for time, often ends up just sending an email announcing the change. And you know how that works out, having been, I'm sure, on the receiving end of more than one email like that. When communicating a big change, sending an email announcement—with the expectation that once the recipients hear about what's going on, they'll miraculously "get it" and everything will proceed smoothly—doesn't work well. It doesn't work for the team leader, who doesn't get the buy-in they need, or for the employee, who doesn't get the information they need to buy in.

Eventually, if it becomes clear that there's not a lot of progress making the change, many leaders respond by just talking more, telling their team members what to do with increasing frequency and volume as their own worry and frustration grows. Once again, this doesn't work well either. Meeting after meeting and week after week, their efforts fall short.

These are skilled, well-intentioned leaders, by the way. They've bought into their organization's change, and all they need is for the people they work with to do the same. So what's going wrong? Why haven't they been able to put change into action despite having a clear goal and directive to do so?

This is usually the point when someone calls me. Leaders are experiencing more of what I'd call "derailing pain" versus the normal discomfort that most change brings, and they want help.

"Why Won't They Just Do What We Ask Them to Do?"

I was working with a very smart strategic leader in the tech sector—we'll call him Brett—and his executive team, helping them get their organization on board with a new strategy. The change was significant and would take several years to implement, affecting many things about how they worked together and how they engaged with clients.

Brett's employees were pushing back against the pending changes, as people often will, and he didn't like that, as most leaders wouldn't. He and his executive team had spent months going through the data, considering alternatives, and making choices they believed would keep the business ahead of their fierce competition. Now he couldn't understand why those who were assigned to implement the solutions were resisting, since from his perspective he'd explained very clearly that if things didn't improve, the company would lose clients and revenue, and that wouldn't be good for anyone. "Who doesn't understand that?" Brett fumed. "I mean, we pay these people, so why won't they just do what we ask them to do?"

Now, I knew Brett cared deeply about his people, but when he set his sights on a goal, that sensitivity could go out the window. He definitely leads more from his head than his heart, as he told me when we first met, "Picking up on emotional cues is not my strongest skill."

And Brett's not alone. Even I—a trained psychologist and executive coach who specializes in guiding teams through emotionally tough situations—can overlook how others might feel if I'm focused on an outcome. I lose sight of the fact that it's *my* goal, not *theirs*. I forget that others, including people on my team, didn't have the same access to information or an opportunity to consider other options, which was critical information that helped me decide to change.

Brett was right about a lot of things. He did pay his employees to do what the organization needed them to do. If his executive team announced a change, in a perfect world, his employees would, well, just *do* it. But this isn't a perfect world, and this successful executive was forgetting one crucial point: his employees are human.

You Are Already a Change Leader

Here's some good news: you've already made thousands of changes that have brought you to this point, and so have the people around you. Well done you! I guarantee you're already doing things in your job that make for good change leadership, which is why you're in a leadership role in the first place.

What else makes you an expert? Experiencing what doesn't work. I also guarantee you've been on the receiving end of bad change leadership, which is basically just bad leadership. Remember what that was like? You didn't have what you needed to buy into the change—the information, clarity, or support—that would have helped you become very open to making the change that was needed. Instead, you got the email announcement, but no one talked with you directly about what the change meant for you.

Most likely, none of the leaders who practiced bad change leadership in your past intended to do so...they might have been just too busy, unclear, or unskilled themselves. But they taught you something through what they lacked, showing you what to avoid.

Here's some more good news: practicing good change leadership doesn't involve changing who you are or starting a whole new set of actions that add to your already busy daily schedule.

What Can You Do?

You can't make people change, but you can influence someone's decision to support a change through what I call *skillful change leadership,* which is:

- first, understanding what information and support people need in order to get on board with a change happening around them, and
- second, providing information and opportunities for open, candid communication with your team, giving them greater control, which makes it easier for them to support the change.

We'll spend the rest of this book exploring those two ideas, in terms of incorporating the priorities that underlie all good change leadership and then through discussing the most common tough change leadership situations, with practical action steps that guide people through accepting and implementing an organizational change.

Thankfully, Brett ended up getting it. How? First, he trusted me enough to believe there was a better way to lead through change (maybe my jumping up and down during a meeting and emphatically expressing "there's a better way to do this" made an impression?). Second, he started doing his own reading on the topic (his curiosity and passion for learning are real strengths). And third, we were able to take theoretical concepts (like you can't change people) and start turning them into practical, concrete actions that he and his team could take. The process Brett, his team, and I created, in fact, became the foundation for this book.

I want to help, so if you're ready to go *forward*, let's get to it.

Chapter 2

Our Brains and Change

What we'll cover:

- Why people will do almost anything to avoid uncertainty
- Neuroscience concepts and what they mean for you as a change leader:
  - Threat of uncertainty
  - Negativity bias
  - Switch cost
  - Analytic and empathetic networks
  - Optimism

Most of us can think of a time when we were blindsided by an email or an announcement about a change. And as we saw in the last chapter, we've all experienced and probably initially resisted some kind of change in work or life, especially if no one really explained it to us or gave us a chance to ask questions or share concerns. Sure, maybe your decision makers set up a town hall or team meeting with a Q&A, but did you want to be *that lone person,* asking the hard question in front of everyone? Or maybe they sent that general announcement email, closing with, "Let me know if you have any questions." (Where to begin?)

Now you're the leader who's in charge of announcing a change, maybe feeling personal resistance to the change yourself, while also needing to help your team understand and adopt something new. There may be a lot of reactions and feelings going on, and even team members who are usually calm and accepting may be pushing back.

What's going on?

Would it help you to know that the reactions you're seeing

are all part of basic human biology?

While an emotional reaction in itself is not a bad thing, there can be bad behavior that results from an emotional reaction that gets ignored, and that's what we want to avoid. Chances are you know the people on your team pretty well. You are hopefully aware of their strengths, quirks, and past responses to change. Yet many leaders forget to use that knowledge before they announce the next change. They also forget (or maybe have never understood) that we humans are quite the paradox when it comes to our ability to make changes.

On one hand, our brains are hardwired with something called neuroplasticity, which allows us to change all the time as we learn and grow. There was a time when researchers assumed our brains were pretty much "baked" once we reached adulthood, but we now know that our brain can continue to evolve throughout our lifetime. Neuroplasticity can step in when a part of the brain is damaged, moving functions to other, undamaged areas, but it also creates the ability to change the physical structure of the brain as a result of learning.

At the same time, humans are hardwired with a primal response that responds to changes as threats, which helps alert us to danger when things in our environment shift. While it's unlikely that some large-toothed, hungry beast is chasing you today, your very literal brain will still respond that way when it senses something it doesn't recognize. Additionally, there's also a human reaction called "loss aversion," which basically means that the brain gives more psychological weight to the possibility of losing something we already have than to the potential benefits of something new, making it challenging to let go of what we know. Both of these hardwired responses can, and probably will, make the people on your team more resistant to changes, which is why your good change leadership will be key to helping them overcome their instincts.

Understanding these natural brain functions will help you, as a team leader, better understand the things I suggest to lead your team through change, but this chapter comes with a disclaimer: science's understanding is evolving all the time as research and technology continue to advance. The brain is also highly complex and integrated, which means as a system it's never linear, so pulling out certain aspects is tricky. I'm going to do my best to keep it simple.

As mentioned, I'm a nerd when it comes to this stuff and would happily learn and talk about brain functionality all day, but you're probably not, so we'll focus here on just five concepts that I think are relevant to helping your team through change:

- Threat of uncertainty
- Negativity bias
- Switch cost
- Analytic and empathetic networks
- Optimism

Your job as a change leader is not to *control* your team's emotions and reactions to change. Your job is to *understand* their emotions and reactions to change and then use that understanding to control how you respond...which will in turn affect how they choose to respond. This mindset is key to your ability to work through every reaction to change, but especially resistance.

Here goes.

Threat of Uncertainty

While I was in graduate school, I designed an 8-week self-awareness and personal growth program for inmates in a county jail in California. I learned a lot during that time, but one experience in particular has stayed with me.

When I first saw Ricky at the start of a new class, he walked with his shoulders hunched and head down, looking visibly defeated. He hardly said a word for the first 6 weeks. I didn't know what crime Ricky was convicted of, as I made it a point not to bias my opinions or behavior by asking anyone why they were in jail. All I knew was that he was awaiting sentencing.

When I showed up to teach the second-to-last class, I encountered a completely different Ricky. He was laughing and joking with others. He looked energized, like the weight of the world had been lifted, so I assumed he got good news about his sentence.

"Elizabeth!" he excitedly said when he saw me. "Guess what?"

I smiled and waited for the big reveal, wondering whether his charges had been dismissed or if he got a light sentence.

"I got 30 years!" He beamed.

I tried not to let the horror show on my face. *Thirty years*?!

Ricky taught me a powerful lesson that day. Having information, even if it's bad, is better than not having any information at all. Most people spend their lives trying to avoid uncertainty. I realized that Ricky's happiness wasn't about his sentence. It was about being taken out of the intolerable, anxious place of not knowing.

When we know what's coming, even if it's unpleasant, our brains can better prepare for it. We have some control over the actions we choose to take in our lives. It's true for the inmate, it's true for your friends and family, and it's certainly true for you and your team.

You probably know someone you could label as a "control freak." Well, when it comes to change, we're *all* control freaks. In fact, one study[1] looked at how we behave—or more accurately, how our brains behave—when we're in a situation with a lot of uncertainty. What the researchers found was that when faced with uncertainty, people become much more likely (actually 75 percent more likely) to overestimate the chances of something bad happening. In other words, what is unknown is labeled as *bad* as opposed to just *unknown*.

What does this mean for you as a change leader? If your team is left wondering what a change means for them, there's a good chance that, like the people in the study, 75 percent of the time they'll assume that it means something bad. Creating their own "data" in the face of the unknown is an attempt to create certainty, but it usually ends up creating nothing but rumor mills. Still, the human desire for certainty is so strong that if left without information, we'll create our own story, even if it's an inaccurate story with a bad ending. This is why frequent, two-way communication is so critical in leading through change, which I'll be repeating again and again!

Negativity Bias

As mentioned, our brains are constantly scanning our environment for anything that could cause harm. But what else contributes to assuming that the change will be bad for us? The research is clear: our brains give more psychological weight to negative experiences than positive ones. As Dr. Rick Hanson, psychologist and bestselling author, says, "The brain is like Velcro for negative experiences, but Teflon for positive ones." He goes on to say, "Negativity bias shows up in lots of ways...The result: a brain that is tilted against lasting contentment and fulfillment."[2]

What does this mean for you as a change leader? When you introduce a change to your team, keep in mind that you are introducing an unknown, and so your team will automatically start to analyze how the change will be bad for them. This reaction is normal—it means they have healthy, working brains—and shouldn't be seen as the team behaving badly. When you work within those parameters, you'll be able to approach their reactions, concerns, and anxieties with compassion and can use your curiosity to ask deeper questions. You can invite them to share and reflect on their concerns, making it more likely that what is unknown will be addressed early and not cause blocks later on.

Switch Cost

Whether you think you're good at quantifying risks and rewards or not, there is a highly attentive and invisible geek living in your brain who *loves* tallying those figures. This tiny geek spends all their time calculating whether the costs of making a change are worth the rewards. For example, I thought it was a great idea to learn Italian while spending an extended period of time studying in Italy, but my internal geek (who looks a lot like the woman wearing horn-rimmed glasses from a Gary Larson *Far Side* cartoon) did not! While my pronunciation was okay, it was mentally painful, awkward, and exhausting to remember the words and rules to put a sentence together. The enthusiastic encouragement of my teacher, fellow students, and the Italian people, who patiently listened as I struggled, was not enough to motivate me to keep up my efforts. In other words, the switch cost was too great.

At work, switching from doing something one way to another requires effort from you and your team. Even if the change makes sense intellectually to you and your team, making the change will still be hard. This is an additional reason people resist change. It's uncomfortable to learn a new process, skill, or technology, which means you will probably be less productive, take longer to complete the task, and make more mistakes. You may feel like a beginner again, like when I was learning Italian. The idea of it was exciting, but actually doing it was problematic. Many of us like staying in the feeling-of-the-idea phase of something versus the action phase, which is where the discomfort of doing becomes real.[3]

What does this mean for you as a change leader? People tend to feel good when they reach a level of ease and mastery in any aspect of their lives, and especially at work. Perhaps they're recognized as an expert, so people come to them for advice. They see a link between their success and promotion, more money, or other recognition, and that makes them feel great. Then you come along with a change that upends what they are doing and creates the need to shift or even learn a new approach. They lose their perceived status as an expert and become a beginner again.

As a leader, your challenge is to use compassion to appreciate what they're losing, while showing them that success in this situation is defined as learning something new versus mastery of the old way, giving your team (and their internal geeks) confidence and reinforcement to make the effort to change. You can also work with them, taking a task and working together to complete it using the new way, helping them move from the idea phase through the steps of taking action.[4]

Analytic and Empathetic Networks

Discussing how to handle emotions and reactions to change usually takes up a fair amount of time when I work with leaders. One memorable moment came from Doug, a sales leader who shared during a group session, "I'm so busy focusing on this change right now I don't have time to worry about anyone's feelings." He was joking, of course, but we all understood exactly what he was talking about. It's not that he didn't care about feelings; it was more that he felt a lack of internal bandwidth to deal with feelings because most of his energy was focused on the goal he was trying to achieve.

Doug perfectly articulated what I'll call the battle taking place in our heads. I have seen it over and over again, between what researchers have called our *analytic network* (AN) and our *empathetic network* (EN).[5] I hope you get a ton out of your investment of time and money in this book, but if you take only a few tidbits, I invite you to make this skill one of them: become aware of which network you are in and then ask yourself if it is the right one for the situation.

Your AN helps you focus your attention, analyze a situation or data, come up with solutions, and then make a decision. Very important as a leader! Your EN, on the other hand, helps you to be open to possibilities, including seeing patterns that help you innovate new ideas. It also helps you be empathetic, picking up on others' feelings and emotional cues. Also extremely important when leading through change! But here's the catch: while both networks are multifaceted and brilliant, research has shown that when one of these is active, it suppresses the other. Oh yeah, learning this one piece of information has explained a lot for me about why leading through change is so hard!

What does this mean for you as a change leader? When you try to lead a change predominantly using your AN, you'll focus on analyzing data, meeting timelines, and achieving goals. Unless you pause and specifically do things that require EN activation, you won't easily pick up on how your team is feeling or recognize opportunities to innovate. This helps explain why great project managers can be so good at tracking the technical details, resources, and deadlines of a change while not being so good at recognizing and responding to emotions and reactions, even though they are still data points, just in a different package.

Depending on your organization's focus, its culture, and your own strengths, you probably favor one over the other. For instance, if creating spreadsheets and analyzing data gets you energized, you probably favor the AN. In fact, most business cultures favor and reward AN functions and activities. Unfortunately, these same cultures want innovation, which ends up getting suppressed in their AN-driven environments. Being a good change leader requires you to go back and forth between the EN and AN, creating clarity and communicating the path forward, providing timelines and success measures (AN), and also responding with compassion, recognizing what's going on for you and the team, and providing a place to work it out together (EN).

Optimism

Neuroscience research tells us that optimism, or feeling good about the future (or a successful outcome), helps us not give in to fear. Using optimism isn't about ignoring difficulties or not allowing for negative emotions; it's a tool that frees a brain stuck because of fear or anxiety. It allows us to see possible ways forward rather than being stuck in all the things that won't work. In this sense, optimism isn't just an end result of something that went well; it's the fuel needed to get better results.[6] I really love that last bit.

What does this mean for you as a change leader? Using optimism, celebrating progress, using humor, and talking confidently about the future will help your team (and their brains) to plan, make better decisions, and take action, especially if they are stuck. In other words, imagining a positive outcome, even if there isn't a clear path to getting or "feeling" there yet, refocuses the brain away from fear. Talking with your team and imagining together what a good future actually looks and feels like, even if you're still experiencing the bad stuff, makes the creation of that future much more possible.[7]

Understanding what's happening in the brain when change is involved has always made me feel better and, surprisingly, usually does the same for the people I share this with. I think it's comforting to know we're in good company: "Oh good, it's not just my team (and me) who reacts like that." Now that you have a foundation on what happens inside our brains during change, we'll take this information and build on it, introducing you to the 3 Priorities great change leaders practice when leading their teams through change.

Chapter 3

The 3 Priorities of Change Leadership

What we'll cover:

- 3 Priorities of Change Leadership:
  - Compassion: Using curiosity and questions to help your team through difficult changes
  - Communication: Sharing good news; plus why saying "I don't know" is so much better than saying nothing at all
  - Clarity: Helping people understand what they need to do differently and sharing what success looks and feels like

I think it's good that I'm hearing more leaders say, "Yeah, yeah, I get that change leadership is important, Elizabeth. Just tell me how to do it!" While there are still leaders and organizations who don't fully get it, we've come far enough that I spend less time convincing people that leading through a change requires specific actions and more time preparing leaders to take those actions in a simple, practical way.

The challenge of sharing something "simple and practical" led me to sift through the latest research on the brain and teams, pull out the important bits, and then articulate these insights into what I call the *3 Priorities of Change Leadership*. No doubt the change will require a variety of actions to become a success, but the 3 Priorities of *Compassion*, *Communication*, and *Clarity* provide a guiding framework for the types of actions to take when leading people through change, as opposed to managing the project aspects of a change.

As a great change leader, you will:

1. Use *Compassion* to consider the perspectives of each member of your team in relation to the change so you can understand what might be difficult, what they may lose, and what they need to succeed.
2. Engage in ongoing, frequent two-way *Communication*, in which you provide information about what is changing and why, while also asking your team to share their concerns and inviting their perspectives and participation going forward.
3. Create *Clarity* between people and the new priorities so they know what they need to do differently in their day-to-day activities to get the new desired results.

While each of the 3 Priorities is unique, they are not linear or chronological. You can't do one and check it off, then move to the next. Complex or difficult changes may require you to "dial up" one priority at certain times, but you need to practice all three. They overlap and are dynamic parts of a whole, systemic approach to change leadership.

I'll get into more detail about practicing them in specific situations in Part II. For now, let's explore each and how they work together.

The 3 Priorities in Action

"Whaaaaat is happening?" I nervously asked my colleague. We were both on a video call with our client, Dimitri, and his team of sales leaders, and while I wasn't in the room to see all of their body language, what I could see and hear told me that the conversation was veering off track fast. I was supposed to be helping them scope their change, discuss resources needed, and then plan how to communicate the change to the rest of the five hundred people in the organization. Dimitri had already had several conversations with his direct team about the change prior to this meeting, and he had assured me that they were ready to move ahead, but that was decidedly *not* what I was hearing.

Change conversations that don't go as expected, like this one, happen frequently and can be "opportunity" moments if a leader recognizes them. If you can pause to listen and engage instead of trying to force your team in a direction, you'll hear important data about concerns or potential obstacles that will get in the way of success.

Sometimes you need to slow down in the moment to move faster in the long term.

While I was still trying to figure out what was happening, Dimitri wisely recognized that this was one of those opportunity moments, and he slowed down. "Okay," he said, "I get that you're not sure this change is a good idea. I thought you were okay with it, but I can hear you're not, so let's take the time now and talk about your concerns."

Instead of ignoring how the team was feeling and pushing ahead with his own agenda, Dimitri engaged their resistance with Compassion, inviting them to share their perspectives and committed to hearing them. Then, practicing Communication, he asked the team to get into pairs and list all the things that could go wrong or that were still unclear to them. He then took the rest of the meeting to discuss what was on their minds. With each specific concern raised, he practiced Clarity, providing more details or, if he couldn't provide an answer, explained what he was going to do to make sure the question or concern would be addressed.

This wasn't lip service to the team either. Dimitri is a driven, yet responsive leader who wanted to understand the issues they were raising—issues that would have blocked the change moving forward if left unaddressed. After all, there would be no change without his executive team being on board and helping to lead the way.

Compassion: Using Curiosity and Questions to Help Your Team through Difficult Changes

Dimitri was actively practicing all the priorities in real time, but that conversation especially demonstrates the priority of *Compassion* because he met his team where they were and tried to see the change from their perspectives. While I could tell that he was frustrated at times because he thought they were past this point and ready to move forward, he never tried to rush them. That extra hour he spent listening, addressing concerns and potential obstacles, probably saved him many hours of additional work later.

These moments happen all the time, but most of us are so focused on an outcome or agenda (operating from our analytic network) that we squander these moments, trying to convince people to get with the program instead of listening to where they are. Many of the leaders I have observed do a lot more "telling" than "asking" (operating in the empathetic network), especially when emotions start to run high.

Recognizing when to pause, express curiosity, and understand how people are feeling, rather than driving ahead, is especially important when you're faced with team members who aren't doing what you want them to do. Here are some signs:

1. *When you find yourself saying the same thing over and over again, with increasing frustration and/or volume*, it's time to stop telling and instead ask an open-ended question (eliciting something other than a yes or no response) to help you and your team figure out what the concern is.
2. *When you are in a disagreement about the change, or some part of the change, with a team member*, it's time to stop debating (telling) and start asking questions and listening to their issue, challenge, or concern.
3. *When you're surprised because your team is not doing the things you asked them to do to support the change*, it's time

to check their understanding of the goal and gain clarity about the action steps or behaviors needed to implement the change.

A simple rule of thumb on whether to *ask* or *tell* is that if you find yourself in a situation where the resistance is based on misinformation or miscommunication, then telling your team the correct information is a good start. If you're dealing with an emotional reaction or resistance even after you've clarified the correct information, chances are it's time to explore what's going on by asking more questions.

Tell/Ask Chart

TELL when someone:	ASK when someone:
Struggles due to missing information or miscommunication	Shares an emotional reaction
Lacks direction because they are new to a task, situation, or team	Expresses words or behaviors that don't align with your expectations around the change
	Has the information and skills needed but still struggles to make the shift to the required new behavior

Going back to the three examples above, let's look at how you might approach a conversation.

When you find yourself saying the same thing over and over again, with increasing frustration and/or volume, stop and ask the team what might be preventing mutual understanding and clarity. Left unexplored, this issue could derail the change.

1. **Frame the discussion**: "Let's pause for a minute, because I feel like we're going in circles, and I don't think what I am saying is helping. I want to make sure I understand what you need so we can figure out how to move forward."

2. **Ask one or more of the following questions**:
    - "What do you think the current issue is?"
    - "Why do you think that's happening?"
    - "Are you clear on why we're making this change and what is expected from you?"
    - "What do you think has been preventing you from moving forward? Is it missing information, lack of clarity, external obstacles, disagreeing with the goal behind the change or a part of it, or something else?"

3. **After listening to the responses, reflect back**:
    - "Thanks for sharing your perspective. I can understand now why this was a problem."
    - "Here's what I have seen/heard…and here is the impact it's having…"
    - "Here's what I see you/me/us needing to shift/change…"
    - "What do you think?"
    - "Are you concerned about anything I'm asking you to do?"

4. **Seek agreement**:
    - "Let's agree that the next step is…does that make sense?"

- "What might get in the way?"
- "What strengths can you leverage to help you? Here's what I have seen you do well..."
- "What's the first step you could take? When will you start?"
- "How can I help/what action can I take?"
- "What's the best possible result we could achieve?"

When you are in a disagreement about the change, or some part of the change, with a team member, start welcoming a different point of view. Become curious about their perspective or concern, trusting that there is wisdom in their reaction, even if it's not immediately apparent to you.

1. **Frame**: "Let's pause for a minute because I feel like we're not on the same page. I want to make sure I understand what you need from me so we can move forward."

2. **Ask one or more of the following**:
   - "As you think about this change, what concerns you most?"
   - "What else could go wrong?"
   - "What do you think might be lost as a result of the change?"
   - "Are you clear on why we need to make this change?"
   - "Is there any other concern you want to share that you don't think I understand?"

3. **After listening to the responses, reflect back**:
   - "Thank you for helping me understand...I get why you are raising this now."
   - "Here's what I have seen/heard...and here is the impact it's having..."
   - "Here's what I see you needing to shift/change..."

(focus on two or three areas at most)
- "Are you concerned about anything I am asking you to do?"

4. **Seek agreement**:
   - "What do you think you can do differently?"
   - "What might get in your way?"
   - "What strengths can you leverage to help you? Here's what I have seen you do well…"
   - "What's the first step you could take? When will you start?"
   - "How can I help/what action can I take?"
   - "What's the best possible result we could achieve?"

When you are surprised because your team is not doing the things you asked them to do to support the change, first check their understanding of the goal, action steps, and expected behaviors as they relate to the change.

1. **Frame**: "I'd like to talk with you about…I want to make sure we are both clear on the outcomes we are looking for and how you, and we as a team, can deliver on them, including how I can help."

2. **Ask one or more of the following:**
   - "Here's what I am seeing/hearing (not seeing/hearing) and it's causing…(or) the impact it's having is…Is this a surprise?"
   - "Are you clear on why we are making this change and what is expected from you?"
   - "What do you think is causing the issue? Why do you think that's happening?"
   - "What do you think has been preventing you from moving forward?" (e.g., missing information, lack

of clarity, external obstacles, disagreeing with the change or a part of it)

3. **After listening to the responses, reflect back**:
   - "Here's what I see you needing to shift/change…" (focus on two to three areas at most)
   - "Are you concerned about anything I am asking you to do?"

4. **Seek agreement**:
   - "What do you think you can do differently?"
   - "What might get in your way?"
   - "What strengths can you leverage to help you? Here's what I have seen you do well…"
   - "What's the first step you could take? When will you start?"
   - "How can I help/what action can I take?"
   - What's the best possible result we could achieve?"

Communication: Sharing Good News, Plus Why Saying "I Don't Know" Is So Much Better Than Saying Nothing At All

There are a number of things that may get in your way when it comes to communicating with your team during change. Here are four frequent comments I hear from my clients:

1. "I don't have all the information yet. I'd rather wait until I have answers so I don't say the wrong thing."
2. "It's a big change, and I don't think the team will react well. I'd rather wait until I'm more prepared."
3. "I don't have a lot of time right now and would rather communicate with the team when I have enough time to do it right."
4. "The change is underway, and while things are going

well, we still have a long way to go, and I don't want to break the momentum."

On the surface, these are all perfectly understandable reasons, and there is some wisdom in each. However, all of these reasons have more to do with what the *leader* wants and needs (to have the answers figured out), not what the *team* wants and needs (information, even if incomplete, to reduce uncertainty).

Let's find the wisdom in each of these and then rework that wisdom to help you respond more effectively using good Communication, as well as Compassion and Clarity:

1. *"I don't have all the information yet. I'd rather wait until I have answers so I don't say the wrong thing."*

Of course you want to have the right information. What if you say the wrong thing and cause more problems? But is it possible there's also something else behind your response? For many of us, it's hard to tolerate the discomfort of saying "I don't know."

Intellectually, you probably know that you can't possibly have all the answers your team will want when it comes to a change. Yet there may still be some part of you that feels saying "I don't know" is unacceptable. I know this is true for me. I still battle that little voice in my head that holds me to a standard of perfection, telling me if I don't know something that means I am doing something wrong, as opposed to it meaning that I lack information or haven't learned how to do something yet. The good news is that when you see this happening, you can take a deep breath and try reframing it, which will be so much more helpful to you and your team. And truly, it's also okay to say "I misspoke earlier. Here is the correct information."

WISDOM 2.0: Tell yourself: "As a leader, my job is to become curious and create clarity where I can, even if I don't have all the answers. It is all right to say 'I don't know.' I can start a conversation and see how many questions or concerns I can get to surface. This means I need to shift my goal from having the answer to uncovering the question or concern. I'll know I am successful when my team has shared all of their questions and concerns, including a bunch that I can't answer...*yet*. As a change leader, I can tolerate the discomfort of not having answers, even apologizing if I did give the wrong information, which will help my team members tolerate their own discomfort with uncertainty and still move forward."

2. *"It's a big change, and I don't think the team will react well. I'd rather wait until I am more prepared."*

A tough change may cause you to feel anxious, sad, frustrated, overwhelmed, angry...and that's before you even start to interact with your team. They're also going to have these feelings, and maybe a whole lot more. Who wants to deal with all of that anger, fear, or anxiety? This is especially true if you're feeling these emotions yourself.

Or maybe you're just tired because there have been a lot of changes and you've been dealing with tough emotional reactions for a long time. Or perhaps you just don't think you're equipped to deal with strong, negative emotions.

Most leaders I know would rather skip dealing with all of those feelings when it comes to a change and just "git 'er done," especially if a change is inevitable. I don't blame them. I do this for a living, and sometimes I'm still overly enamored with my analytic network, ignoring the emotional side of change management in a misguided attempt for speed and efficiency.

Yet similar to the example above, once you recognize what or who you're avoiding, you can make a more thoughtful choice about how to respond. When you or your team are not on board with what's happening, those normal emotional reactions can sabotage your best efforts and increase the very strong possibility that the change will fail, which isn't a great outcome if you are accountable for the result. And the only way to know if they're on board, or to help them get there, is to start the conversation.

WISDOM 2.0: Tell yourself: "As a leader, my job is to be courageous and go first when we are in unknown territory. I can share with my team that I also have some anxiety, concern, or frustration about this change and why so that they know these feelings are not a problem. This means I need to shift my goal from avoiding or fixing emotional messiness to starting a conversation to understand how the team is feeling, accepting their feelings as normal, and then creating clarity where I am able."

3. *"I don't have a lot of time right now and would rather communicate with the team when I have enough time to do it right."*

I appreciate that you're trying to be thoughtful, wanting to give time and attention to your team and not rush through important conversations. But I'm going to be direct with you. I don't think this is the main reason most leaders don't communicate enough. I'm sure you're busy, but can you point to a great leader who isn't? Are there other reasons for not talking with your team about this change? Acknowledging them will help you all move forward.

You already know that not communicating now will cause more time-consuming problems you'll need to fix later. You probably also know that communication becomes easier if it's frequent and comes in shorter bursts rather than saving everything to share all at once. Twenty-minute individual or team huddles or stand-ups are enough to provide quick updates, celebrate successes, or surface an obstacle that can then be addressed in the right way, with the right people, at a different time.

WISDOM 2.0: Tell yourself: "As a leader, my only job is to enable my team to succeed, and they will succeed only when they have the information and resources they need to get the job done. Once I discover what's preventing me from communicating, I can use my existing meeting schedule or have shorter team huddles to find out what my team needs to know. I might not have a lot of time or all the answers, but I do have time to ask one question: 'What's on your mind about this change?' This means I need to shift my goal from communicating everything to *communicating in moments* where my team and I focus on one thing that matters most now." Pretty soon, all those moments add up to great communication.

4. *"The change is underway, and while things are going well, we still have a long way to go, and I don't want to break the momentum."*

The Communication Priority of change leadership is not only about *how* you communicate (using two-way communication, as you've heard already) but also about *what* you communicate. Many leaders have every intention to communicate with their team frequently during change, but then things get in the way.

"People are desperate for good news," Mara told me while we were in the midst of leading her team and organization through a recent change. Unfortunately, she told me, she'd learned this one the hard way. "At my last company, I didn't pay enough attention to my team's feelings and need for communication along the way. I left a trail of unhappy people. I'm not doing that again. I know now how important it is to recognize people and celebrate their successes."

Her comment reminded me of a meeting I once attended, where the company's CEO came to talk to his team about his vision for and perspective of a transformation effort already underway. "There's some positive client feedback," he said, which was great to hear. But then he added, "This doesn't mean that we can take our foot off the gas pedal. There are still things we need to fix, and we still have so much to do." He started talking more about what was going wrong, detailing many of the issues that were still not "fixed" and how changes were not happening fast enough. Only after sharing all that was still wrong did he share the positive client feedback.

The thing was, his comments about the need for improvement were absolutely right. We all agreed. But I still walked away knowing that he'd missed an opportunity to support and motivate his team through the change. After that meeting, two things became clear to me. First, a leader communicating good news is a powerful way to keep people engaged. It's hard for employees to see all of the positive impacts of the changes they're implementing from where they're sitting. They don't have the whole picture. The staff in that meeting already knew how far they still had to go, but hearing that clients were experiencing the benefits of the team's hard work gave everyone a much-needed lift. Their efforts were paying off, which gave them the motivation to keep going.

Second, it's often hard for a leader to pause and share good news midway through a change. There's always something that should be fixed, another problem to solve, another client who could be happier. I think some leaders fear that if they say "great work," employees will stop driving the change forward.

Leaders get paid for a variety of things, and finding and fixing problems is at the top of the list. But leaders aren't the only ones who want to find and fix problems. Most employees also want to help. They're on the front lines, making them acutely aware of issues that create pain points for clients or customers, as they're the ones fielding the unhappy calls. As a change leader, if you focus most of your time on what's wrong or what still needs to be fixed (staying in the AN), you are missing a really easy way to keep people energized and engaged (using your EN) while the change is still underway.

That's not to say you should stop trying to improve, but take the time along the way to let your team know that they're doing things that are making a positive difference. Celebrating successes helps people keep going. It offers a ray of light in the middle of a dark tunnel or a glimpse of the finish line at the end of a long race. To keep making the effort to change behavior (the switch cost we talked about in the last chapter) and remain engaged as obstacles arise, your team needs to know that their efforts are working. Research shows that celebrating large and small successes, which we'll talk more about in Chapter 9, helps people remain positive, and a positive attitude helps the team solve problems, learn, and remain resilient.[8]

WISDOM 2.0: Tell yourself: "My team needs me to continue to hold the bar high so we can achieve great results. Continuously improving helps me, my team, and the company remain competitive. To help them continue to do more of "what's working," I can celebrate their successes along the way, recognizing behaviors that help us move the change forward, helping them feel optimistic and energized, which we'll need to overcome obstacles that arise."

Clarity: Helping People Understand What They Need to Do Differently and Sharing What Success Looks and Feels Like

This one seems obvious, right? How can people actually make the change if they don't know how their behaviors and actions need to change or what success looks like? Yet clarity is one of the most frequently overlooked areas of change leadership. Sure, some lack of clarity is normal during change, but the problem is that what is clear often just doesn't reach frontline employees responsible for implementing the change.

My clients frequently share their frustration about team members who don't make the necessary behavioral adjustments needed for the change to succeed, but often there's a disconnect with what the team leader and team members think is necessary. I remember one training session I was conducting where a team of leaders talked about their "difficult employees" who just wouldn't do what was needed to move a change forward. They had communicated the change and invited their team members to share their concerns. So what was the problem? As the session continued and we talked about creating Clarity, the light bulbs started to go on. They realized that they had talked with their teams about the *mechanics* of the change and had received their feedback (well done them!) but hadn't talked with individual team members about the *specifics* of what each person actually needed to stop, start, or continue doing each day as a result of the change. The team wasn't trying to be resistant; they just didn't know what they were supposed to do differently.

Sure, there are "difficult" employees out there who won't do what they need to do even though they have the information. But most employees simply lack clarity about what a change means for them. This is made clear in a study that bestselling author Marcus Buckingham and the ADP Research Institute conducted across 19 countries to measure engagement, specifically those factors that were most likely to attract and retain talented employees. Their results showed that one of the most important factors in building an employee's trust with their leader (trust being *the* most important factor in retaining talent) is: *Do I know clearly what is expected of me at work?* Their data indicated that those team leaders who helped their team members gain (or regain) clarity on specific priorities and what was expected of them, even in the midst of changes, were more likely to have a fully engaged team.[9]

In other words, people need you to tell them what they are supposed to do. There is a fine line here, however: clarifying *what* a team member needs to do differently as a result of the change is not the same thing as telling them *how* to do it. (Although sometimes the how is also necessary if they are new to the task or are encountering an obstacle that they need your help to remove.) Buckingham says, "To do this, give your people as much accurate data as you can, as often as you can—a real-time view of what's going on right now—and a way to make sense of it, together. Trust the intelligence of your team."[10]

Together is a key word here, as it is with all things related to change leadership. It aligns with what we learned in Chapter 2, helping people move from the idea phase of a change to taking action to move the change forward. Working together with individual team members, or the team as a whole, and actually walking through tasks—breaking them down into smaller pieces and applying the "new way" to complete the task—can reduce anxiety and produce results. When you're faced with implementing a complex change, you need the full force of your team's collective brain power focused on moving the change forward together, without being drained by confusion or anxiety.

I'll share a specific framework to help you do more of this in Parts II and III. First, though, we'll focus on you and how you feel about the change, as all good change leadership begins with the change leader, then move to some playbook examples to help you talk with and lead your team through changes.

Part II
Communicating the Change

So far, we've been talking about change and leadership in general terms, exploring the principles, science, and experiences that are common in a variety of situations.

But you're probably not facing change as a general concept. You're probably facing a specific change. You probably picked up this book because you are leading, or soon will be leading, your very own challenging change situation, and you may not know what to do or where to start.

That is the focus of the rest of this book: to make a tough change as easy as possible for you by offering specific coaching, step-by-step guidance, strategies, and tools that you can apply right away.

If you're at the beginning of a change process, start with the information in Part II. Chapter 4 will help you prepare (don't skip this; it's an important step!) to talk with your team. The general playbook in Chapter 5 will help you communicate almost any kind of change to your team, but some changes are harder to lead through than others. And so in Chapters 6 and 7, you'll find specific scripts and additional actions, tools, and advice for handling two of the toughest, and yet most common, changes in business today: the ones that involve job losses and the ones that come as total surprises, often before you—or anyone—can finalize a plan.

If you're already in the middle of a change and have questions about how to handle midstream challenges, you may want to skip ahead to Part III, though reviewing the playbook steps in Chapter 5 could also help you identify any missed steps that could be causing some of the challenges you're facing now.

Whatever kind of change you are facing, consider it an opportunity to practice the 3 Priorities of Compassion, Communication, and Clarity. Your confidence and capabilities will continue to build with every experience you navigate, and at some point, you won't need this book anymore because you'll have mastered the fundamental skills needed for any change situation. Notice when this happens, because it will, and celebrate these moments!

Chapter 4

Start with Yourself

What we'll cover:

- All emotions are good emotions
- Primary emotional reactions to change: on board, uncertain, or resistant
- What to do when you're not on board
- Naming your feelings
- How to choose a more helpful perspective and reframe your thoughts

Hopefully by now you're convinced that the emotions bubbling up around the change are absolutely normal reactions that deserve our attention. However, I understand that *normal* certainly doesn't mean *easy*.

I remember one situation where the difference between leaders who made time to address feelings and reactions and those who didn't was, quite literally, written in black and white. I conducted a very lively "leading through change" session with a client, where leaders were given time to understand the change itself, ask questions, share concerns, and also prepare for tough questions they might get from their team.

As a post-session action, we gave the leaders a framework to use when they discussed the change with their teams. While we considered making this a mandatory step, we ultimately decided that wasn't necessary. We assumed (our first mistake) that the leaders would naturally all talk with their teams about the change because they were now better prepared and, well, they *were* team leaders. Talking with their team was part of the job.

Fast-forward 3 weeks, when we received the feedback from our first anonymous employee survey about the change. We were shocked! Only 30 percent of respondents answered "yes" to the question, "My manager has talked with me about the change." The remaining 70 percent of employees, the ones who responded negatively to that question, went on to express mild annoyance to flat-out rage in the optional comments section. "No one bothered to talk with us, which is so typical." "This is the worst change yet. How could anyone come up with such a stupid idea?" "The management of this company has no clue what we frontline employees do...they are completely out of touch!" I left out the expletives.

Here was direct evidence that the leaders who talked with their teams about the mechanics of the change *and* invited their feelings, reactions, and concerns made it more likely for employees to get behind the change quickly rather than resist it. It was also a great lesson in how many will avoid having the uncomfortable conversation, especially if the change is a tough one.

So while it's tempting, it's a bad idea to ignore feelings—both your own and those of others—when leading people through change. In fact, addressing the emotions—both your own and those of others—is the *first* thing you need to do when you find out about an upcoming change, and here's why: **our emotions trump our rational thinking, especially when it comes to creating change and making decisions.**

Brain science confirms that unexamined or unconscious negative feelings (especially anxiety) disrupt our thinking brain. In his book *Your Brain and Business*, Dr. Srini Pillay writes:

> Anxiety centers in the brain are connected to short-term memory, risk-benefit analysis and attention...Specifically, we now know that our brain's emotional system:
>
> - Has direct connections to the brain's action system and, thus, the ability to change behavior

- Influences how/when we decide whether or not making the change is worth the effort
- Impacts our ability to focus and learn new things ...When (we) are anxious, (our) decisions may be impacted.

In other words, unexamined emotions can derail thinking, taking over when you least expect it and causing havoc.

I am sure you have experienced this yourself. Emotions can sneak up on you in the form of frustration or irritability, cause delays when unexplored resistance leaks out slowly in the form of procrastination, or show up forcefully in conflict between those who are trying to move the change forward and those who are not on board.

While you might not be able to control your team member's decision to change, taking time to examine feelings before they come out in surprising or negative ways is something you can control. The key to working with your emotions through a change—for myself, the leaders I work with, and for you too—is to *identify*, *examine*, and *address* feelings before they lead us into a giant mess.

When It Comes to Change, All Emotions Are *Good* Emotions

In case I haven't said this often enough yet, there is *no bad emotional reaction* to a change. I've met many leaders who think about their team's reactions, especially the negative ones, as a barometer of how good or bad their own change leadership skills are. They think: if people are resisting, I must be doing a bad job.

In fact, it's likely that you and your team members will feel a variety of emotions, both positive and negative, over the course of the change, and these will be completely out of your control. The team may like a change where they are given the lead on an important project (yay!), but those feelings turn into frustration when a key team member leaves a couple of weeks later and can't be replaced because there's a hiring freeze, creating more work for everyone (argh!).

What's more (and here's why there are no bad emotions), wisdom can often be found in negative reactions, both yours and those from your team, if you treat them as something to be understood, not dismissed. Emotions are data, as valuable as any numerical statistic on a spreadsheet. You might have the collective will to make a change but still feel frustration if you're lacking resources to get it done. Surfacing that frustration can lead to a solution, either getting the head count or shifting priorities, as opposed to ignoring the feeling and then getting derailed at a future point.

While there are no bad emotional reactions, there can be bad behavior that results from an emotional reaction that's unexamined or ignored. These can take the form of visible resistance, like when a person engages in actions that are out of alignment with what's needed to move the change forward. Resistance can also be more passive, which is harder to spot. Someone may dislike the change and not say anything, even as they start looking for a new job. People in these positions are often externally compliant, going along with proposed changes without really being on board or enthusiastic.

Remember: your job as a change leader is not to *control* emotions and reactions to change—and that includes your own. Your job is to *understand* emotions and reactions to change. Bringing emotions out into the open prevents those feelings from exerting influence from the shadows. Or, to put it another way, once you understand your reactions and any emotion that's behind them, you can probably do something about it.

Primary Emotional Reactions to Change

While people can have a variety of reactions to change, in my experience the main emotional reactions can be simplified into three general categories: on board, uncertain, and resistant.

Let's take a look at the value in each of these three reactions.

When someone is *on board*:

- Their support increases the overall momentum for the change.
- They are ready to receive and take on change-related activities.
- They can influence other team members to get on board.
- They spend time talking about what they like about the change and where they see benefits.
- They are more likely to see obstacles as temporary, not as a sign that the change is a bad idea.
- They can be a good audience for you to talk to and test your messages.

When someone is *uncertain*:

- They challenge you to clarify what the change means now, on a day-to-day basis, and in the future.
- Their hesitance can provide the opportunity to pause and check any assumptions about how the change is being implemented, including what else needs to happen before continuing to go forward.
- They will probably act with a deeper commitment when they see the value of the change.

If you have more than one team member who is uncertain, you may need to work on building trust, providing additional information, or addressing "change fatigue" (especially if multiple changes are underway).

When someone is *resistant*:

- They can help identify important problems that need resolution.
- They'll provide information and feedback that can strengthen your communication.
- They will press you to address concerns and potential obstacles before you implement change.
- They will be more likely to ask the tough questions, if given a safe opportunity to do so, which can improve implementation and results.

Are *You* on Board?

Now, think about a current change you are leading or need to lead. You know what the change is, even if you still may need more details. You also know it's going to happen. So at this point, how do you feel about it?

Pause for a few minutes here to consider the following statements. Which one best describes your current attitude toward the change you're leading?

"I'm on board."

- I understand why the change is being made and, for the most part, believe it makes sense for my team or organization.
- I have enough information to move forward.
- I have enough clarity on what is expected.

"I'm uncertain."

- I'm not sure I fully understand why the change is being made, and I'm unclear about whether it makes sense for my team or organization.

- I don't have enough information to move forward.
- I don't have enough clarity on what is expected of me or my team.

"I'm resistant."

- I don't understand why the change is being made. In fact, I think it could be a bad idea for me, my team, our clients, and maybe the organization as a whole.
- I'm pretty sure I don't have all the information I need to move forward with the change presented, but given what I do know, I think it's a bad idea, and I can tell you a number of reasons why.
- I might have clarity on what's expected, or I might not, but it doesn't really matter because I think it's a bad idea.

If you are mostly on board, you're ready to start planning. Feel free to skip ahead to the next chapter. If you're feeling any resistance, uncertainty, or some combination of the two (which is pretty normal), then keep reading. It's time to get clearer on what you're feeling and what to do about it.

Name Your Feelings

If you're having a less-than-positive reaction to a change on your horizon, this is a great time to explore those feelings. This doesn't have to take a ton of time, but it does require some focus and self-honesty. At this point, it doesn't matter if your feelings are rational or welcome. Suspend any judgment for now and use your curiosity to discover what's there.

This is an important step, so don't dismiss it. As we saw in Chapter 2, your emotions are not just fluff. They are hardwired into the brain and impact outcomes. They are an important source of data, even though they are not in the form of words or numbers on a spreadsheet. Also, chances are if you're feeling uncomfortable about an upcoming change, your team will too, so understanding your own emotions will prepare you for working with feelings your team members may have.

If you're reluctant to admit to your feelings, remember that you don't have to tell anyone else how you feel, but by telling yourself, you'll be able to focus your precious time and energy in the right direction to figure out what to do about it. In other words, don't waste energy judging the merits or acceptability of your feelings. None of your emotions are a "final state"; they will shift as you explore them, adjust, and get new information.

What are some things you're feeling? Here are some examples from my own emotional "naming and claiming" when I wasn't on board with a change: "I'm not happy with this change." "I'm frustrated." "I'm confused and uncomfortable." "I'm overwhelmed."

Why might you feel the way you do? It's in the *why* that you'll discover the wisdom that will help you and your organization figure out what might be needed to move forward.

- I'm not happy about this change because I think it will be bad for my team, the department, and my career.
- I'm frustrated because my expertise has been ignored, and that leaves me feeling undervalued.
- I'm uncomfortable because I am not sure the person making this change really understands the problem we are trying to solve.
- I'm overwhelmed. While I agree with this change in theory, there are already a number of changes in flight that are taking a lot of time and energy from me and the team.

Turns out these feelings are very common. In the leader training sessions I facilitate, I ask participants to remember a time when they resisted a change. I ask them not to focus on the change itself but to share why they resisted. In almost every session, I hear some version of the following:

- No one bothered to ask or include me in the decision, even though I have the expertise and it directly impacts me and my team.
- We tried this type of change before, and it didn't work.
- I don't understand why we are making this change.
- The change won't be good for me or my team.
- I like things the way they are. We're doing well.
- This change doesn't make sense. It's the wrong thing to do.
- There have been so many changes happening that we're getting burned out.

Sound familiar?

The good news here is that you can work with all of these reasons for resistance in a productive way if you choose because there is wisdom in each reason. *You can have mixed feelings and still move ahead.* Let's examine each of these common responses, recognizing the wisdom in each, to help you choose how best to respond.

No one bothered to ask or include me in the decision, even though I have the expertise and it directly impacts me and my team.

Yes, there is wisdom in feeling upset that your expertise was not sought out because you probably do have something valuable to offer. It's hard when others make decisions that impact us, yet we aren't included. But ask yourself, do you believe that not inviting you to the discussion was malicious, or was it a consequence of how most organizations function these days—overwhelmed by too many priorities and not enough time to speak with everyone to understand the impact of their actions or decisions?

If you have something valuable to offer and would like to be heard, reframe your resistance toward finding a way to make what you want to say worth hearing. In other words, manage your frustration and provide information that will be helpful and make it more likely that colleagues (and your boss) will hear what you say now and in the future.

We tried this type of change before, and it didn't work.

This is common, especially when change comes after a new leader takes over. Your wisdom here comes from not wanting to waste time and effort on something that hasn't worked in the past. On the one hand, you may find yourself experiencing a version of the movie *Groundhog Day*, watching the same things happen over and over. On the other hand, you might not. Have circumstances internally or externally changed? Does the individual or team sponsoring this change understand the problem better, or do they just not know the history?

If it's the latter, look for ways you can offer information so they can learn from the past and avoid pitfalls that could negatively impact the success of the ultimate goal. If your impression is that the people making the change decisions are aware of the organization's history, then it will be important for you and your team to understand what's different this time, or at least why it seems like a better idea now, in order to move ahead with more confidence.

I don't understand why we are making this change.

In my experience, not understanding why a change is happening is the number one reason people resist a change. If it describes you, the first thing to know is that there's wisdom in your instinct to not move forward when you don't understand the landscape. That's your basic survival instinct kicking in—well done, human!

Similar to what was said above, though, reframing your frustration is easier if you can look for and assume positive intent. In most cases, no one is intentionally keeping information from you; they probably just got busy and didn't realize they weren't communicating well. It's time to manage your irritation and respond by having a thoughtful conversation with your boss, colleague, or change sponsor, sharing your concerns while giving them the benefit of the doubt, so you can ask questions and get the clarification you and your team need.

The change won't be good for me or my team.

Your wisdom here comes in caring for and protecting yourself and your team. That makes you a great leader! This is a tough one for leaders, though, because some organizational changes are good for the organization in the longer term, but, in the short term, leave individual leaders and teams feeling sidelined—or worse, facing job losses. If the change you're facing seems to negatively impact those closest to you, step back and look at the bigger picture for a moment. Is it better for the organization? Are market conditions necessitating this change? Does it create efficiency or a better customer experience?

It's great when you, the team, and the organization are all aligned. Unfortunately, with the pace of change these days, misalignments occur more frequently. The goal of reframing in this case is to accept that you and your team can implement changes that are in service of the broader organization. Not everyone can do this, but if you can, you'll be rewarded. It's a small world out there, and handling the experience with grace and maturity will give you a reputation as a leader who is willing to put aside your individual interests and do what's best for the whole.

I like things the way they are. We're doing well.

There is wisdom in appreciating when something is working

well, including being ready to talk about *why* something is working for the company or clients, not just because you like things how they are. While there is nothing wrong with liking things as they are, it doesn't make for a clear business case.

At the risk of telling you something you already know, it's important to mention we all have to implement or go with changes we don't like, especially when we're part of an organization. Early in my career, I got frustrated when I had an idea or saw an opportunity to do something better but the organizational leaders (my bosses) decided not to do it or to do something I thought was not as good an idea. In these moments, a favorite mentor of mine used to say, "Elizabeth, you're not wrong. But until your name is above the front door, you need to decide if you can influence the current decision, and if you can't, you need to let it go and move on." It was a frustrating response—frustrating because I didn't like it—but I knew she was right. Maybe your leaders are seeing and needing to respond to a market condition or other factors that you and your team can't see. So approach your manager with curiosity, assuming that there is information you don't have access to that might be informing the current need to change.

This change doesn't make sense. It's the wrong thing to do.

There is definitely wisdom in sharing your concerns about an upcoming change. Your company pays you to share your expertise through honest and open communication (at least I hope they do). And the leaders who will implement the change need this data, especially if you see real obstacles and challenges coming.

Be thoughtful in how you share your concerns, though. Take the time to evaluate and understand your reasons. Then, if you share them and the decision makers still want to move ahead, it's time to shift your mindset. Yours is one perspective, and there may be information you and your team don't have that helps the change make more sense. How can you move ahead with this change, doing your best to account for the challenges and continuing to communicate when an obstacle arises? It won't be good for you or your team to directly or indirectly block movement.

There have been so many changes happening that we're getting burned out.

The pace and speed of change has been relentless for many leaders and teams, especially in the last several years. Even if you put aside all the "regular" company changes happening, everyone has been dealing with the additional emotional and physical demands brought on by the global events that began in 2020, putting even more people at risk of burnout.

Your wisdom here comes from being a good leader, working to balance the needs and well-being of you and your team with company goals and deadlines. Burnout is basically a result of chronic stress, which leads to exhaustion or even cynicism, plus an inability to focus, which makes people feel ineffective, leading to even more stress. A perfect vicious circle. A number of articles written about how to manage this specific situation are available online, and I'll address ways to help build resilience in Chapter 9. Similar to the advice in the above examples, your goal is to kick off a conversation with your boss (or change sponsor) articulating your intent to support the change and your (and your team's) desire to get to a good result, while being clear about the current obstacles to achieving that result. Come prepared to share ideas on changing current priorities or timelines, where you need more internal support and external resources, and any current roadblocks that are adding to the problem. Bringing these forward, along with stating your desire to support the change, can help create a workable solution.

When You're Strongly Opposed

But wait. What if your emotional reaction is more than "I'm not happy" or "I'm concerned"? What if you are morally, ethically, or otherwise *strongly* opposed to the change that is being asked of you?

That's happened to me. Without going into a lot of confidential details, there was a time when part of my job was to get feedback from a senior executive's team, manager, and peers about what it was like to work with him in order for him to develop. We agreed that this feedback report would be shared only with the executive, an external coach, and me. About a month later, I heard through the grapevine that the head of the company wasn't happy with this executive. Then my department's leader (my boss's boss, in fact) asked me for a copy of the feedback report. He wanted to use it to support a case for terminating the executive.

Yeah, not good!

While not a large-scale organizational change, this was a smaller change that had big consequences I couldn't support. Honoring commitments like confidentiality is *really* important to me. I knew I'd rather quit than go along with this change, which would mean acting in a way that would betray my internal client and my values. I needed to say no. As you can imagine, saying no to my boss's boss didn't land so well. The point is this: while I couldn't control the situation, I could control my response. The department leader never saw the report, and I left the company a few months later.

If you're in a similar place and you conclude that you are morally, ethically, or otherwise opposed to a situation or change, it may be time for you to exit from the situation and move on, as well. Sorry, wish I could offer a different solution for this situation. It's one of the difficult things about working in organizations. Sometimes humans make bad decisions that impact us. Sometimes they make decisions that aren't bad but end up taking the organization in a direction we can't go.

I take a lesson from the Stoics that has helped me shift my perspective, and specifically Marcus Aurelius, as offered by Ryan Holiday from his Daily Stoic website:

> Instead of telling ourselves we're unfortunate because our expectations were disappointed, we should do the opposite. [In the words of Marcus Aurelius:] "No, it's fortunate that this has happened and I've remained unharmed by it—not shattered by the present or frightened of the future. It could have happened to anyone. But not everyone could have remained unharmed by it."...We are only harmed when our character is affected. We're only harmed when we let go of what we believe in or when we drop our own standards. It might not be desirable to lose money or a friend, to fail at something or to be criticized, but how does that make us unfortunate? We haven't been deprived of our ability to respond. Our character remains intact.

I think any of us who have been in this situation before know that it may end with us leaving, but taking time in advance to examine our feelings and response options gives us time to wrap our heads around what leaving will mean and create a plan for what's next. We get to choose how we respond, which begins with choosing our perspective.

Choose Your Perspective

As I shared in Chapter 2, during graduate school, I developed and led a personal growth class to help incarcerated men and women build better self-awareness and hopefully make healthier choices for themselves and others. I'd begin each new class with an invitation for participants to shift their perspective to create more possibility by saying, "The only thing being controlled right now is your physical freedom. No one controls your intellectual, emotional, or spiritual freedom, unless you let them."

This is definitely one of those "healer heal thyself" situations, because I, too, need the reminder that I can choose my perspective. When I am in the grip of fear or angry about a change that I didn't initiate, this is the phrase that pulls me back out. Even if others are behaving badly and my emotions are running high, I can still choose how I think about and respond to a situation. And so can you.

Most of the leaders I've worked with have struggled with this at some point, especially when they're faced with something they don't like or aren't 100 percent on board with. As we learned in Chapter 2, there is a natural emotional pull to go down a path of negativity because our brains give more weight to negative thoughts or feelings. The neural pathway carved by past experience is well-worn, and it will feel normal, even strangely satisfying, to head down the "negativity path" again, in part because it's a way of trying to gain some degree of control. *At least we are doing something*, the thinking goes, even though in reality that *something* isn't helpful.

That *perception* of reality, though, *becomes* reality, and a negative reality can be very limiting. The key to moving forward is to recognize which thoughts and emotions are depleting your energy, making you feel worse (and maybe making those around you feel worse too) rather than helping you move in the direction you want to go.

Perception is the dictator of experience. If you are approaching an upcoming change from an anxious or negative perspective, take time *before you talk to your team* to reframe your own thoughts to something more empowering, while still feeling authentic. Before you go further, write down your current perspective and then practice shifting it to something more empowering to help you feel strong in this situation.

Here are a few examples of what an empowered perspective might sound like:

- "While I may have mixed feelings or lack all the details about the current change, I can talk with my manager or change sponsor to address my concerns and get additional information, including understanding what is not known at this time. I don't have to be 100 percent on board yet to start leading through this change. Instead, I can thoughtfully communicate my concerns to get them addressed, which will help me support my team with concerns they might have, as well."
- "I can't control anyone's reaction to the change, but I can take time to prepare for my team's tough questions and emotional reactions so that I will have a better chance of responding in a way that's helpful to them."
- "My job is not to make people change. My job is to use Compassion, Communication, and Clarity to help my team decide to change and to provide the support and resources they need to be successful. I will focus on understanding what my team needs by asking them, sharing information as soon as I have it, and helping address and remove obstacles as they arise."
- "I may not have a ton of experience leading through change, but I have the resources, including people and information, to figure it out. I've learned and mastered many new challenges before this, so I will figure this out as well. Instead of needing to be an expert, *I will focus on being an open, curious, and willing learner* and on using each situation, including the tough ones, to practice and celebrate trying something new."

Remember, you are the only one who can decide to stop, shift your perspective, and try something else. You have the power to understand why you feel the way you do rather than acting like everything is fine.

Leaving the company that wanted me to break a confidentiality agreement could have seemed like something unfortunate, like the Marcus Aurelius quote above. But it turned into something else entirely, because I landed my dream job with an amazing leader and team. Things were going well for a couple of years, until the economic crash of 2008.

The name of that company with my dream job? Lehman Brothers. Enough said.

But that fact brings me to the final step: reframing your thoughts. If you find yourself resisting a change but not, as in the above situation, strongly opposed to it, then you're ready to take the next step. You've identified how you feel and why; now you can look for ways to shift your perspective to match your new reality.

Reframe Your Thoughts

As you can imagine, being at the epicenter of the financial meltdown of 2008 brought up another series of changes for me, with plenty of opportunity to get stuck in fear. How would I survive? But I'd learned enough to know that fear wouldn't help me figure out what to do next. Instead, I chose to follow the steps in this chapter: to pay attention to my feelings and recognize when fear was taking over and why, to take deep breaths, and then to practice shifting my perspective and reframing my thoughts, consciously stretching myself to see the future, and different possibilities, in a more optimistic light. Changing perspective may not work all the time, but it actually has worked more often than I thought.

To shift your perspective you need to reframe your current thoughts. Reframing is the art of shifting your emotional state using language and questions to create a different focus and, thus, a different emotional experience for yourself. It's moving from asking questions like "Why is this happening to me?" to asking "If I imagine this situation is perfectly designed for me and my development right now, what can I learn?" When you're facing a change, look for a way of thinking about your current situation that strikes the balance between healthy caution and a hopeful picture of what's possible in the future. You don't have to like it to move through it successfully.

In my Lehman Brothers example, my first step was to pause when I was feeling anxious and recognize the current fearful thought. "I'm not going to get another job in time, and I'll end up running out of money."

Then I'd try to reframe that thought to something less dire but something that still had truth in it. Here's what worked most of the time: "I've always landed on my feet in the past, and while I don't know exactly what's next, or every step to get there, chances are I will find another job...maybe even something better." That would stop the downward plummet into fear, which then allowed me to choose what I wanted to focus on instead. And this was the perfect design for my own growth; I struggled with anxiety, so it was a chance to practice not letting it take over.

Because I was not stuck in fear, I was then able to shift to another empowering thought, "What can I actually do now with my energy, things that are in my control, which will put me in a better position in the future?" One thing I did was to take steps to manage my finances in case I had a prolonged period of unemployment (which happened), and then I focused on being of service to others around me who needed my help, which made me feel stronger and better, another resilience-building strategy proven out in neuroscience. I worked on my colleagues' resumes, introduced them to my network, listened when fear got the better of them and provided encouragement (because I could empathize), and then celebrated with them when they found new jobs. And while this last one would trigger my fear a little bit again (and some envy too) because I hadn't found a job yet, I'd notice this feeling, honor it as truth, and start practicing the cycle all over again.

Lastly, I opened myself up to many supportive friends, who were generous with their time and encouraging with their words. Not only did I give to my network but I also received a huge amount of love and support! I had always felt more comfortable with giving than receiving, so practicing receiving support was also helpful for me. Having their support would remind me how lucky I really was, and I'd feel gratitude and then optimism, another powerful antidote to fear or anxiety because: "When you have hope and optimism, you have an automatic way of replacing fear in the line of emotions asking for attention from the amygdala. That is, hope and optimism decrease the emotional distractions that affect thinking…it actually impacts how your brain searches for solutions."[11]

Doing these things isn't easy! And I had to repeat this cycle over and over again (and still do). We all have moments when the stress, anger, or fear gets the better of us. That's okay; it happens. In these moments, another quote that helps me is from author and artist Mary Anne Radmacher: "Courage doesn't always roar. Sometimes courage is the quiet voice at the end of the day saying, 'I will try again tomorrow.'"

Putting It All Together

We've explored a lot here, and because starting with yourself is critical, I am going to summarize the key points to help you see specifically what you can do right now—or at a future date, if you don't want to reread this chapter but want a quick refresher.

1. *Name your feelings*. Are you currently on board, uncertain, or resistant to the change that's coming? Pause and treat your feelings as important data that will either help or hinder you as you make the change. Spend less time fighting your feelings and accept them for now. You can't shift anything that you are not willing to acknowledge and accept. Acceptance doesn't mean complacency,

agreement, or a final state. It just means seeing what is as *what is* for now.

2. *Figure out why you feel the way you do.* Trust that there's probably a good reason you are feeling the way you do. What are your feelings trying to tell you? What's the wisdom in your feelings? What's the good intention behind your negative feeling or thought? Maybe it's protecting yourself, trying to prepare for or help you avoid the worst? Our negative thinking is often our ego's attempt to warn us of impending danger. The problem is when we treat this perspective as a certainty, as opposed to a future possibility, we close off to other possibilities, including better ones.
3. *Choose your perspective.* Remember, you choose the meaning of a situation. This isn't about being "Pollyanna." It's just you exploring different options. For example:
   - "Maybe something better is possible since I don't know everything right now and don't have the power to predict the future."
   - "There have been times in the past when I imagined the worst-case scenario, and in many of those cases, it turned out better than I thought, or I was re-directed to something better, even if it took a while."
4. *Reframe your thoughts.* Use questions to help you come up with alternate possibilities. For example:
   - What are facts versus assumptions in this situation?
   - Is my perspective the only possibility?
   - Is there a more optimistic or empowering perspective?
   - What strengths can I bring to manage this situation?
   - When I've experienced something like this before, what did I learn that I could apply here to help me or others?
   - What have I learned from others who have moved

through difficulties with both realism and grace?
- What are the aspects of this change that I can control?

Taking the knowledge you have gained about yourself and how you feel about the change, you are now ready to prepare to talk with your team. Chapter 5 will help you take steps to prepare and, when you're ready, help you talk with your team about the change.

Chapter 5

How to Communicate a Change

What we'll cover:

- Forward Change Leadership Playbook:
  - Understand the impact of the change
  - Identify strengths
  - Prepare for tough questions and reactions
  - Envision success
  - Create your message
  - Have a team conversation
  - Follow up

While good organizational change leadership is about more than communication, launching a new change and getting your team on board is *all about* communication. This seems so obvious, yet in my experience, communication is the number one thing that breaks down when an organization launches a change. And boy, does it make people mad! Think about those times when change was happening around you and you weren't clued in. When this happens, we start creating all sorts of reasons why no one is telling us what we need to know, and none of our thoughts are very forgiving.

I like to remember Hanlon's Razor when it comes to organizations and communicating change: "Never attribute to malice that which is adequately explained by stupidity." Okay, that's not very compassionate of me, I know, but it's usually true (and kind of funny, which helps me lighten up a bit when I am in those situations). In my experiences with leaders, I've never known anyone who was sitting there giggling maniacally and thinking, "I'm not going to communicate about a change because I want my people to fail." Instead, as we've seen, issues with communication usually happen because the leader is focused on just getting it done (operating from their analytic network) or they feel they don't have the time, right words, or answers, which is really about their fear of saying something that would upset the team. It can be especially hard if the leader is not entirely on board yet themselves and they understand, or even agree with, what they're anticipating their team might say.

When leading your team (and I mean your direct reports) through change, keep reminding yourself that *your job is not to make other people change*. Take a deep breath and read that again. I hope it makes you feel a little bit better.

However, you do still need to get a change moving forward. Some changes feel relatively small, without any obvious direct impact to your team. Yet even small changes can cause concern.

So let's look at the things you *can* do—which, in many cases, are things that you are probably already doing in some way. I call this the Forward Change Leadership Playbook because it's a step-by-step guide to using the 3 Priorities of Compassion, Communication, and Clarity to more easily and effectively communicate an upcoming change to your team. There are even scripts and sample slides!

Before you dive into these steps or start talking to your team, make sure you've been through the questions and exercises in Chapter 4 so that you understand where you're coming from personally. Then let's get started leading through change.

Forward Change Leadership Playbook

1. Understand the impact of the change

Some changes are bigger than others, but as we've seen, no change is easy. One leader I worked with said, "I am always surprised about people's reactions to a change. Even when I don't think it's that big of a deal, someone on my team does." That's an important reason why leading with Compassion can make a huge difference when you need to announce a change.

Before you get too far into the details of creating your messaging, step back and identify what might make this change difficult for your team. What, exactly, might you or they have trouble with, and why? What might they be losing? Use the prompts below to help you think in more detail about the impact. Consider writing down your responses. (If you want to track your journey right in this book, there's space for that in the Forward Change Leadership Tool, found in Chapter 10.)

- One thing that will be challenging for my team in this change is:
- Another challenge for me or my team will be:
- Implementing this change will mean my team will need to start, stop, or continue which activities or tasks?

Identifying the impact of this change is particularly important when there are other changes at play. We all wish we could live in a magical place where changes happen one at a time, in logical sequence. But that's not the reality of organizational life (that's not the reality of *life* either). Changes are constant and can be contradictory, causing your team members—and you, often—frustration and fatigue.

Here's an example of how important it is to consider the scope of a change. One client hired me to help him and his executive team lead through a change in strategic direction. In preparation, we met as an executive team and outlined the scope of the change together, including how this change impacted and was impacted by other projects and initiatives happening across the company. Seeing how many changes were already "in flight" in his business unit was such an eye-opening experience that this new executive shifted what he was asking me to do to support the company; he realized that the first priority would be creating a session where every leader in his department could weigh in on the importance and progress of each change already underway. The result was a greater alignment on which changes would continue and which would be tweaked or stopped altogether, plus a candid conversation about the impact of all of this on frontline employees. That then resulted in further adjustments to reduce or better align the various change initiatives going forward.

Here are some additional questions to help you consider the impact of this specific change on your team:

- Do any aspects of how we work together or communicate need to change, even if only in the short term?
- What processes, workflows, or technology must be reconfigured as a result of the change?
- Will my team need to learn any new skills to be successful in the future?
- How does this change intersect with or influence existing changes underway?

2. Identify your strengths

Once you've identified the general challenges, shift your perspective, and make a list of all of the experiences, skills, characteristics, and abilities that your team will bring to this change effort and how those will make the change successful. These thoughts will be important to share with your team to help them choose or shift their own perspectives about the change.

For instance, maybe a team member has a technical skill that will be needed. Or maybe someone is really good at building team spirit, helping inspire others when things get rough. This is not about ignoring the deficits or challenges you'll face; you made a list of those in the first step already. It's about recognizing the things that will help people feel strong in order to not get stuck in anxiety. Reminding yourself and others of their strengths, especially those gained through past changes, helps people feel more confident as they approach a new one. Include your own strengths in your answers to the prompts below.

- One strength I/we bring to this change situation is:
- Another strength I or my team brings to this situation is:
- A past situation where we used our strengths to move through a change successfully was:
- Strengths that we used then that really helped were:

3. Prepare for tough questions and reactions

Leveraging the list of challenges you identified in step 1 and the insight that comes from Compassion and empathy, consider the specific emotions or other reactions each member of your team may have when they hear about this change. In particular, this is a time to prepare for those who will feel a loss of some type. While you can't predict every person's response, it's probably safe to assume that you will face some initial resistance. After all, if something is changing, something is ending for someone.

If you need some additional help with this, start with completing the **O.U.R.** (on board, uncertain, or resistant) **Team Assessment**, outlined below. There's a blank form in the Forward Change Leadership Tool, found in Chapter 10. This will help you anticipate and prepare for the tough questions or reactions you may face, while also figuring out who your early adopters and helpers might be.

Engaging in a discussion isn't about deciding whether anyone's feelings are right or wrong; we've already seen that all emotions are good emotions. This is about being aware of and open to your team's individual needs and reactions, incorporating Compassion (accessing your empathetic network) into your response as a leader by not getting thrown off or surprised.

How to Use the O.U.R. Team Assessment

Directions:

1. Write the names of each team member in the first column.
2. Consider the approaching change from each person's perspective. What could be the consequences, or the perceived consequences, for this specific person? Write that in the second column.
3. In the third column, write down how that person might initially feel about the change.
4. In the fourth column, consider what they might need from you to get on board with the change. This could be one of the 3 Priorities or something tactical like skill development/training.
5. Lastly, given what you know right now, would you consider them to be on board, uncertain, or resistant to this change?

Here are two examples:

Change: the current manual workflow is becoming a fully automated, digital process

Team member	What might happen to this person as a result of this change?	How might they feel?	What will they need to make the change?	Initial reaction: on board, uncertain, or resistant?
Tia	Losing a way of working/ being an expert in a process. She will need to learn a new process.	She might initially be frustrated because she helped create the original workflow process, which she performs well.	Invite her to share her frustration or concerns —I need to listen—and use Compassion to empathize with her feelings, which make perfect sense from her perspective. Affirm the importance of her skills and strengths and discuss how those will be used in the new process. Ask what she would need from me to move forward with greater confidence.	Resistant

Change: the team is moving to a different location

Team member	What might happen to this person as a result of this change?	How might they feel?	What will they need to make the change?	Initial reaction: on board, uncertain, or resistant?
Jacob	Moving from the westside office building to our eastside office.	Lives much closer to the eastside building. He might be very happy about this change!	Basic information and timing. Other than that, I don't think he'll need to be convinced to make this change.	On board

You are likely to hear concerns and tough questions as you introduce this change, both in your wider team conversations and in your one-on-one discussions. After you have completed your O.U.R. Team Assessment, use those insights to also write down any specific questions or concerns you expect to hear from your team.

Every change situation is different, but here are the three tough questions (and some variations) that I've seen come up, in some form, every time there's a change:

1. Why do we need to make this change when things are going well?

2. What will the change mean to me?
    - Is my job at risk?
    - I really enjoyed what I was doing before the change, so how much of my job will be different now?
    - Will I have to take on more work?
    - What does this mean for my career?

3. What if I disagree with the change?
    - We have tried before and failed, so what's different?

As you think about how to respond to these questions, keep the following guidelines in mind as you use the 3 Priorities (Compassion, Communication, Clarity) in each conversation.

- **Be authentic in your responses**. If you were uncertain about this change at first, be honest about that, including agreeing with or acknowledging the validity of their concerns, comments, or feelings.
- **Actively listen and affirm** what people are saying or asking, appreciating that even tough questions show they care.
- **Ask a clarifying question** to give the team member the opportunity to share more before you respond. With a particularly tough question or a team member who is clearly resistant, this approach will give you more information so that you know you're responding to the *real* question. It also has the added benefit of giving you more time to think, while helping your team member feel heard, appreciated, and understood.
- If questions come up in a team gathering, you can **invite other team members to respond first**. They may have a perspective that can help, especially if they are on board, and you'll get a better idea of how widespread a concern is.

When the tough questions are expressing uncertainty or resistance, here are some prompts for ways you can start thinking about your answers to questions in one-to-one or team conversations:

- *"That's a great question. I can share my thoughts with you, but given what you know about the change so far, what are you thinking?"* Again, before you jump in, get some more information from the person asking the question. They may not have all the information, may have misunderstood what's been communicated, or simply need the time and space to share what's on their mind.

- *"At this point, here's how I/we are seeing the impact on you..."* Be as specific as you can about the impact you see on the person's current job, including their main focus areas and work priorities, including what they do on a day-to-day basis. Address any of the related questions as directly as you can.
- *"Given what I've shared, what impact do you see? What concerns you at this point?"* Depending on the change and their question, you can also ask:
  - "What is unclear?"
  - "What might be gained as a result of the change?"
  - "What might be lost as a result of the change?"

Respond to their concerns, including saying "I don't know" if you don't know. Try to always acknowledge when someone raises a good question/point, and commit to getting answers back to them if you don't know right away.

If the employee is having a stronger emotional reaction, listen and show Compassion by saying things like:

- "Yes, that makes sense. What else are you feeling?"
- "If I am understanding you correctly, I hear your concerns are..."

Ask if the person would like some time to reflect on what you discussed and then meet again, or if they want your help in solving their concerns now. The challenge is not moving into problem-solving or advice-giving mode until they have had the time to fully articulate their concern and process their emotional reaction.

Once they are ready to move into problem-solving, you

can begin with questions to help your team member explore a different, more empowering perspective:

- What are the facts versus assumptions you have about this change?
- What outcome are you concerned about? Is this the only possibility?
- What could be a positive outcome?
- What could you or we do to make that outcome more likely?

Make sure each team member understands that just because they don't have all the control in this situation doesn't mean they don't have any. Help them focus on what they can control, namely the choices they make in response to the change. Here are some additional questions that may help:

- What's one thing you can do now to help the change move forward?
- What could you/we start working on that would make the biggest difference?
- What would success look or feel like?
- How can I help you?

4. Envision success

Now that you have a clearer sense of how your team might react, create a positive vision of success. As we saw in Chapter 2, neuroscience shows us that if we're not focusing on a positive vision of the future, we can get stuck in the experiences of the past. Having a vision of a successful outcome activates the possibility circuits in our brains, creating a path for forward movement. People have an easier time making a change if there is something inspiring to aim for rather than just a problem to fix.[12]

So before you announce this new change to your team, prime your brain with possibility thinking and then take action.

Imagine you have been successful in leading your team through this change. Practice seeing and feeling success as clearly and fully as you can.

Here are some prompts to help you imagine your success:

- What has been accomplished?
- What or who are you particularly proud of? Imagine the person who might have the most resistance at the start becoming one of the most valuable contributors to success.
- What obstacles have you overcome?
- What does your team say that you did that helped them be successful? See their smiling faces, imagine the meetings and conversations where you are all reflecting on your success together, sharing stories, laughing, and talking about all the obstacles you overcame.
- What benefits have you achieved for the team, the organization, the clients, and other stakeholders? What are they feeling, expressing, or experiencing?
- What are you feeling as you imagine your success? Relief? Happiness? Gratitude? Satisfaction? Physically feel these in your body and heart area as fully as you can. Let the thought create the experience, which is what primes your brain for this possibility to become a reality.
- Lastly, sum up your thoughts from the above questions and create a one-to-three-sentence statement that captures a *positive future vision* of this change for your team.

Reminding yourself and your team about this positive future vision gives you something to aim for when you start to get weighed down by doubt or anxiety. Concerns can be good warning signals to pay attention to but aren't good as a baseline from which to operate day-to-day. Remember, negative thoughts are not reality; they are just a possibility, so don't give them more power than they actually deserve or mistake an anxious thought for a reality.

I love Mark Twain's take on this: "I've lived through some terrible things in my life, some of which actually happened."

5. Create your message

I can't tell you how often the leaders I have worked with have set out to launch a change with their team without a simple, one-page message that focused on what the team needed in order to accept and support the change. They had a lot of information, but they didn't know how to share it in a way that mattered to the people who would be affected.

I saw this so often, in fact, that I started asking every leader I worked with: Do you have a clear, brief message about this change that you can share with your team?

Here are the most common responses I heard:

- *"Yes, here's a PowerPoint deck and a high-level, one-paragraph description that those who initiated the change gave me."* I needed to explain to them that their answer was actually "no" for what I was talking about. Multi-page presentations and high-level statements are good to use at some point but not helpful in giving the team information that's relevant for them or for creating a two-way conversation.
- *"I do."* But then those leaders would start talking to me about their view of the change, emphasizing different aspects of the broader organizational vision and message. This is also a good start because they are thinking more about what it means for their team, but still "no" since it's residing in their head.
- *"I'm not sure. What do you mean by a clear, brief message?"* This is my favorite response (I'm not being sarcastic here).

What *am* I talking about?

Whether your change is large in scope or small, centers on technology or people, or involves process or procedure, the first and most important thing every person on your team will need to understand is this: "What will change for me?"

The change message (or statement) you create specifically for your team should take up no more than one page, and it should answer all four of the questions that will matter most to your team when first hearing about a change:

1. What's changing?

2. Why is it changing now, and what happens if it doesn't change?

3. What will the change mean to me/us, and what needs to be done differently?
   - What will be gained?
   - What will be lost?
   - What new actions, behaviors, and results are we looking for (what needs to be done differently)?

4. What benefits will we/I get from supporting this change? (For example, there may be benefits for clients and the organization as a whole in the short or longer term, but also consider whether there are specific benefits for your team and their professional and personal development.)

Your organization might already have a broader change vision or message, which may or may not address the specific questions above as they relate to your team. If it's available, use the organizational message as a starting point, but be prepared to go deeper to make your answers more specific. Answering these four questions together, at the beginning of your conversation, will make it easier for your team to understand the details and nuances of the change and will give them a foundation from which to ask questions without overwhelming them with too much information.

You may have answers to some of these specific points now, while others may still be unknown or need to be figured out in partnership with your team or manager. Be sure to write down your answers, either in the Forward Change Leadership Tool at the back of this book or in your own note-keeping system, so that you can refer back and add to the information as needed. Keep your responses short. See if you can stay focused and fit all of your answers on a single page. This is just the beginning. You can elaborate further during your conversations.

6. Lead an initial team conversation

Now you're ready to actually start the conversation about the upcoming change with your team. I use the word *conversation* here intentionally because it needs to be two-way. You will be sharing your change message, but you'll also be *asking for* and *listening to* their feedback.

This can happen on a large or small scale, a few people at a time or team-wide. Depending on the nature and scope of the change and your organization's culture, you may need to speak to certain team members individually before the group conversation. For instance, if this is a change that affects an individual's job, title, or who they report to, seek guidance from your manager and HR (human resources) partner as communication needs to be coordinated to support those that are losing their jobs as well as those that will remain. (If the change affects job losses, refer to the specific advice in Chapter 6.) As a general rule, talk with your manager about your change communication plan before you talk with your team to make sure your manager agrees on the best way to do this.

Depending on the difficulty of the change and your team's reactions, this announcement may need multiple conversations.

For instance, if the change involves adjustments to employee benefits or day-to-day culture expectations, more conversations may be needed, in coordination with your boss and HR partner. Use your judgment here to consider the impact of this specific change on this particular group of people. The key is that everyone on your team hears a consistent message about the change.

The following conversation guide is designed to help you help your team understand the change, hear their reactions, and talk through and agree on a communication plan that will support you all as the change progresses.

Overview:

There are five parts to this team conversation:

1. Welcome and review agenda
2. Introduce the change
3. Invite the team's perspective
4. Discuss and agree on a communication plan
5. Gain commitment and review next steps

Timing:

The total time needed for this initial conversation will vary, but I have found that teams of up to ten people need about one-and-a-half hours to process through most changes, scheduled in either one meeting or two.

One 90-minute meeting:

- Welcome and review agenda: 5 minutes
- Introduce the change: up to 25 minutes
- Invite the team's perspective: up to 25 minutes
- Discuss and agree on a team communication plan as the change proceeds: up to 25 minutes
- Gain commitment and review next steps: 10 minutes

Two meetings, 45 to 60 minutes each:

First meeting:

Follow the agenda up to and including "invite the team's perspective." Give yourself 5 minutes for a wrap-up at the end, encouraging the team to reflect on the change further, and let them know that you'll be continuing the conversation at your next meeting.

- Welcome and review agenda: 5 minutes
- Introduce the change: up to 20 minutes
- Invite the team's perspective: up to 30 minutes
- Wrap-up: 5 minutes

Second meeting:

Pick up again at "invite the team's perspective." Make sure you still have 5 minutes for a wrap-up at the end, encouraging the team to reflect on the change further, and let them know you'll continue the conversation in your regular individual and team meetings.

- Welcome and pick up the discussion of the team's perspective, including the themes from the last conversation or revisiting the specific details of the change itself: up to 25 minutes
- Discuss and agree on a team communication plan as the change proceeds: up to 20 minutes
- Gain commitment and review next steps: 15 minutes
- Wrap-up: 5 minutes

You can adjust the timing and specific details that you share, given what your team needs, but try to follow the agenda topics in order and don't skip any topic areas. Keep time or ask a team member to help you with this.

Meeting Guide for Announcing Change

Welcome and review agenda:

You can use the text below as the opening of a slide deck if you decide to use one.

> **Welcome**
>
> Today we'll:
> - Discuss our change
> - Talk about your perspective on the change: what excites or concerns you and what information and clarity you need
> - Agree on a specific, go-forward communication plan/strategy to help us move through this change

Timing: 5 minutes

Purpose: Setting the context for the conversation and reviewing the meeting agenda

Key messages/directions: This section is more *tell* than *ask* or *discuss.*

Say:

- "I wanted to bring you all together to discuss a change that is happening. (Name your change.) I want to make sure you have the information and support you need to make the change successful."
- "This is the first of ongoing conversations we'll have as a team."
- "So here's what we'll cover today..." (Read bullets for the agenda.)
- "I really want you to be candid and feel comfortable sharing any questions or concerns you have. How you

feel is important information if this plan is to succeed. I'll be keeping track of any concerns that are raised today and will also reach out to others for answers if I don't have them."

Introduce the change

Timing: up to 25 minutes

Purpose: Share your change message and have a more detailed conversation about the specifics of the change.

Key messages/directions: This section is more *tell* first, then *ask* and *discuss* once they have the initial details. Review your change message, touching on each of the four questions and their answers. Pause to check for understanding and answer questions as they arise. Have any notes or prepared responses ready as tough questions start to come up.

Say:

- "Okay, let's spend some time discussing the change in more detail. I realize this is not an easy change to make." (If the team is already aware of the change, you can acknowledge that or add anything else here that is relevant to your context.)

Then share your change message. I suggest you use a visual here if you have a slide deck, filling in your answers in bulleted points. Remember, keep it higher level on the slide, and then get into more detail in the conversation.

What's changing?

- Why is it changing now, and what happens if we don't change?
- What will the change mean to us? (You may have answers to some of these specific points now, while others may still be unknown or need to be figured out in partnership with your team or manager.)
- What will be gained?
- What will be lost?
- What new actions, behaviors, and results are we looking for? What needs to be done differently? (Again, you may have answers now, or you'll need to figure them out in partnership with your team or manager.)
- What benefits will we get from supporting this change?

Say:

- "Now we're going to review our change in more detail. Again, I know you will have questions, so please let me know as they come up, and I'll address them as best I can. If I don't have the answer, I'll get more information and get back to you."
- "Also, keep in mind that as the change progresses and we learn from experience, how we manage the change and what we do may shift."

Invite the team's perspective

Timing: Up to 30 minutes, depending on which meeting structure you're using (one meeting or two.)

Purpose: Get concerns, emotions, issues, losses, benefits, and the like out on the table.

Key messages/directions: This part is more *ask* and *discuss* than *tell*. Your goal is not to solve problems at this point but to get your team to share what's on their mind.

Creating psychological safety is critical to surfacing honest information and responses. If trust is high and your team tends to be very open and candid, you can either have your team members reflect individually on the questions and then debrief in a group conversation, or you can break people out into pairs or trios. Breaking people into pairs or trios is a better option if trust isn't as high, so comments or concerns don't get attributed to one person. For example, two people take "What concerns you?" During the group debrief, the pair list the concerns they discussed, then other team members add to that answer. If you have a smaller team of four or fewer people, you can do this for the first two questions and then answer the other two as a group.

Additional conversation tips:

- If you prepared for tough questions, then have those and your responses ready to use. You can even say, "Yes, I am glad you asked that because it's one I was hoping would come up. I even prepared for it in advance!"
- There are really only two questions here: "What excites you?" and "What concerns you?" But I've learned that rephrasing them using *gained* and *lost* elicits more information as people consider the change in different ways. Also keep in mind that "What might be lost?" isn't always a bad question. For example, losing extra manual work to complete a task isn't a bad outcome, though getting there may take more effort initially.
- Capture different themes as they arise. If you break people out in pairs or trios, ask them to capture their answers in an email that they can send to you, or capture in a chat window or shared screen if the meeting is held virtually.

- Remember, your goal is to surface as many concerns or questions as you can.
  - Reassure participants that their reactions and questions are normal and that you really want to hear their views and won't take concerns as resistance. There are no bad questions. Share that from your perspective, "resistance is just a concern that has not yet been addressed."
  - Welcome people's emotions. Your job is not to fix or change people's reactions but to listen and find out what they need in order to move forward with more confidence.
  - If there is hesitancy from the group, it may be helpful for you to go first and share some of your concerns or as yet unanswered questions, letting your team build on that.

Say:

- "Now that you have information about the specific change, I'd like you all to take 5 minutes and write down a couple of your thoughts on…" (Read the slide bullets.)

As you think about this change, what:

- Concerns you most?
- Excites you most?
- Might be gained as a result of the change?
- Might be lost as a result of the change?

After 5 minutes of individual reflection and notes, you can open the conversation up to the group.

Say:

- "Let's hear responses to the first question (if it was assigned, let that individual, pair, or trio go first). We're not solving problems yet, just getting this information out on the table. As far as I'm concerned, the more questions and concerns we can raise, the better."

After the team shares their initial responses, open up the conversation to the rest of the team:

- "Okay, what concerns does anyone else want to add?" (You can chime in if there is a concern you also have.)

Next, solicit responses to the other three questions:

- "Is there anything that's exciting about this change, even though it may be difficult in the short term? (There may or may not be answers given here, especially if it's a really tough change.)
- "How about potential gains?"
- "What might we be losing?" (Again, encourage all feelings to be shared. Show empathy and understanding. "Yes, that makes sense.")
- "Thanks so much for your candor." *(Highlight any key themes, issues, and concerns that you will come back to in future discussions.)*

At this point, you can wrap up if you are doing this in two meetings or continue on with team communication planning. If you wrap up, identify what will happen in the next meeting so they know what to expect.

Our team communication plan

Timing: Up to 30 minutes

Purpose: Agree on a communication plan for the next 90 days. More frequent communication is critical to help people get the information and clarity they need to make the decision to get behind the change.

Key messages/directions: This section is more *ask* and *discuss* than *tell*. Let the team tell you what they need!

Say:

- "Given the change and some of the concerns raised, it's important that we have a more focused plan for communication, so let's spend time creating a plan."
- "Because this is new, I want you all to be able to share challenges or obstacles quickly so you can be successful. Let's think about how we communicate for the next 90 days. Then we can evaluate what we need going past that point."

Communication

- What communication practices do we need to add or change going forward?
- Team communication: In what way and how often do we need to meet?
- One-on-one communication: Are additional one-on-one meetings needed, and if so, with whom?
- Discussing challenges: What will encourage or get in the way of surfacing problems?
- How will we know if our communication plan is working?
- What evidence will there be of success?
- What evidence will there be if we are not communicating well and how will we resolve this?

Review each of the questions above as a group and get their input. You may be able to make agreements on communication practices in the moment, or you may need more time to reflect on what's needed. Either way, make sure the team comes to an agreement and then put the practice in place. Discussion prompts are below:

- What type of team communication do we want in addition to our regular team meeting?
- What about one-on-one meetings? Are any meetings more important given the change or timing?
- How will we surface and discuss challenges as we implement this change? Face-to-face? When is email okay?
- How will we ensure concerns come up openly rather than behind the scenes? What will help you feel more confident in raising a concern or challenge?
- If our communication plan is going well, how would we know? Get answers from the group.
- How will you all know if our communication isn't working?

Wrap-up

Timing: 15 minutes

Purpose: Confirm key learnings and themes that came out of the session, and review commitments around surfacing concerns directly and communication going forward.

Key messages/directions: This section is more *ask* and *discuss* than *tell.*

- Get a key learning from each team member.
- Discuss any next steps that you and the team may need. Next steps could include following up with answers to questions, scheduling the next meeting or huddle, holding more team sessions like this, or whatever else the team deems helpful.

Wrap Up

- One key learning
- Our commitments
- Are we clear on frequency and mode of communication?
- Answer: "If I have a concern about the change or see an obstacle, I will . . ."
- Next steps

Say:

- "What is a key learning for you today?" (Share your own experience as well. Everyone can respond, or if you are meeting as a large group, pair people up to do a quick 3-to-4-minute share.)
- "I'd like us all to answer the question 'If I have a concern about the change or see an obstacle, I will...'" (Get a personal commitment from each team member about how they will handle any concerns or uncertainties that arise. The goal is to avoid people keeping these to themselves, which could lead to resistance or them directly or indirectly blocking the change.)
- "Thank you all for your time. I'm looking forward to continuing the conversation on..." (Set a date when you will get back to people regarding unanswered concerns and questions.)

7. Follow up

After your initial meeting(s), continue communicating about what the team needs to do differently on a day-to-day basis as a result of the change. Set aside time to speak with each team member individually so that you can check your impression of their stance on the change, giving them an opportunity to share with you why they are on board, uncertain, or resistant. Do they lack information? Is there an obstacle they see that will prevent success? Once you have the information and understand why they feel the way they do, you and your team member can decide how to proceed.

In general, if the person is:

- *On board*: Get them involved in the change right away, and discuss how they can help support and influence the team to move forward.
- *Uncertain*: Continue regular communication to uncover and address concerns and help them move forward.
- *Resistant*: Ask them to share their concerns and clarify what's getting in their way, then agree on next steps, including continuing the conversation.

Remember: During every change, something is ending for someone!

If you want to understand what could be experienced as a loss, particularly during tough changes where people might be losing something important to them, use the Loss Analysis Tool, which I'll introduce in Chapter 8. It highlights several of the most common types of losses people experience. Again, loss that is unaddressed is more likely to cause resistance. We'll be getting into more detail about dealing with resistance in Chapter 8, when the change is underway and you are not seeing the behaviors, actions, or other indicators that tell you your team is on board.

Chapter 6

When Change Involves Job Loss

What we'll cover:

- Forward Change Leadership Playbook for Job Loss
    - Coordinate with your manager, HR partner, and legal partner
    - Understand the impact of the change
    - Identify strengths
    - Prepare for tough questions and reactions
    - Envision success
    - Create your message
    - Have a team conversation
    - Follow up

How to Lead Through Job Losses

Leading a team through job losses is one of the toughest, if not *the* toughest, change situation a leader will face. Whether the purpose of the change is a reduction in staff or the consequence of another, broader organizational change, it's going to cause a lot of anxiety, both for those who are let go and also those who remain on the team. But at one point or another, most leaders are faced with the reality of this kind of change.

If you're in this position now, you're going to need to manage not only the logistics of a shifting team but also your own and other people's emotions about the loss, including fear, anger, and sadness.

One leader I worked with, let's call her Aanya, learned the department she led was being disbanded. Everyone on her team would lose their jobs, and it was her responsibility to tell them.

Can you think of an easy way to communicate that? Neither can I.

Aanya had two choices. She could keep the news to herself for as long as possible and avoid having people quit early. Or she could tell them up front, which would not only give them time to adjust and prepare but also risk valuable team members leaving before their projects could be finished.

Many leaders in Aanya's position choose the first option, and you can probably understand why. Their knee-jerk reaction is to assume the people on their teams will have their own knee-jerk reactions, find another job, and hand in their resignations, leaving the leader in the lurch. That reaction is totally understandable, of course, but often the leader still needs their team to help the change succeed.

I was working with Aanya at the time, and we talked about the pros and cons of telling the team immediately and of waiting. We brought in her HR business partner to give Aanya details about the assistance and support available to members of her team who would need to find new jobs inside or outside the organization, as well as the retention bonuses for those whom she needed to stay until closing.

After weighing the options, none of which got Aanya excited, she concluded that the right thing to do was to tell the team what was going on as soon as possible. "I am taking a risk by talking to you about this," she admitted to them at the start of the meeting. "You might leave tomorrow. You might even quit today. I wouldn't blame you. For some of you, that may be the right decision. But I'm telling you this because I respect you and care about you. I want to honor your need for information and time to adjust to this massive change and to start planning for your next step."

Whoa.

Slowly, their initial shock began to shift into emotions, which led the team to start asking questions. Using Compassion, Aanya listened to each one and responded as best she could. "I am upset and sad too. I've loved working with this team and our clients. I am still processing what this means for me as well."

When questions came up that she couldn't answer, she said, "There are things I can tell you because I have the answers. There are things I can't tell you because I don't have the answers, or I just can't tell you because the organization is not ready to make certain information public. But I'll tell you as much as I can right now and promise to keep you updated as soon as I have answers that I am able to share. In the meantime, I'd like to hear more about how you feel and any other questions you have."

Toward the end of that first meeting, Aanya practiced Clarity and shared more details about the support employees would get to help them find their next role and some specific next steps she would take with them, including actions to increase the frequency of their team communication. These included:

- Twenty-minute huddles at the end of each day to capture questions and hear what was on their minds, including concerns and any obstacles, plus following up and providing answers to questions they had already asked.
- More frequent one-on-one check-in conversations specifically focused on individual needs, including openness about job searches. Aanya committed to being flexible and giving team members time to pursue other opportunities while they still got the work done.
- Team meetings with consultants from the company's outplacement partner, who could talk about job searches, interviewing skills, resume building, and networking.

Did her team storm out? No. Were they in shock? Yes. Yet they understood that she respected their right to know certain things and that some information just wasn't available. As she spoke, they nodded.

What became clear was that most of the team preferred to hear the truth sooner rather than later. They agreed that the change was the right thing to do for the company and clients, even though the short-term impact on them was painful. They also appreciated having time to openly look for their next gig while still employed.

It helped a lot that Aanya's team was committed to their clients and colleagues and wanted to do what they could to help make the transition successful. When we reflected together a couple of weeks later, Aanya told me that most of the team felt a greater sense of trust with her because she'd made herself pretty vulnerable to them by communicating early. It was more important to her to do right by them than to risk her own comfort.

This is the irony around change communication: most people prefer to have information, even if it's bad, because getting bad information that's clear is better than no information. It creates the certainty our brains crave. Armed with information, people are more resilient than we give them credit for.

The challenge, then, is for the leader who has to communicate the change—that's you—to tolerate the discomfort of sharing tough information when they can't fix it or control the reaction. It's important to trust the wisdom in emotions (even if they are hard to bear in the moment), knowing that if given attention, respect, and time, the emotions resolve themselves. Difficult emotions and reactions become a problem only if they are ignored or glossed over.

Change is an emotional problem wrapped in a business context, and the urge to avoid confrontation is an example of that. Recognizing that you might be avoiding a tough conversation is the first step. From there, you can make a more thoughtful choice about how to handle the situation. There certainly may be times to put off or delay a tough conversation, particularly if there is a bigger communication plan within your organization, but make sure you understand *why* you're doing it. Taking a few minutes to think about and prepare for specific reactions or emotions, including your own, will give you greater confidence going into any conversation.

Forward Change Leadership Playbook for Job Loss

When it comes to leading through a change that involves job losses, the overall set of steps that we saw in Chapter 5 remains the same, with one addition at the beginning.

1. *Coordinate with your manager, HR partner, and legal partner*

Since I don't know the specifics of your situation, let me offer advice that may be obvious: before communicating *anything* about job loss, coordinate with your manager regarding what and how you will communicate with your team to ensure your communication is aligned with any broader organizational messaging and actions.

If you work in a larger company, your legal or HR department will most likely be involved, so keep in close contact to make sure what you do aligns with their messaging and timing.

2. *Understand the impact of the change*

With a change like this, you may be able to sum up the impact in two words: *it's bad.*

Okay, noted.

When changes have been made, especially difficult changes that include team members exiting, the people losing their jobs will feel bad, and so will those remaining on the team, who will feel empathy for those colleagues who are losing their jobs and also concern about whether their job is at risk. You should be prepared to address these concerns in your messaging.

For now, think about the different things that might be challenging and write down your responses, either in the Forward Change Leadership Tool in Chapter 10 or in your own note-taking system. I've included some questions from Chapter

5, plus some others that are more specific for this situation:

- One thing that will be challenging for me in leading through this change is:
- Another challenge for me or my team will be:
- Implementing this change will cause my team to lose:
- What aspects of how we work together will need to change?
- What work will need to be moved/absorbed by those remaining on the team?
- What processes/workflows must be reconfigured as a result of the change?
- What knowledge, skills, abilities, or client relationships will be lost or need to be transitioned? What training is required and for whom?
- How does this change intersect with, or influence, existing changes underway?
- Will my team need to learn any new skills to be successful in the future?

3. *Identify strengths*

You may be feeling sad about or even dread leading your team through a change that involves job losses. These feelings are real and can inform how you lead, especially in having Compassion for others who are feeling the same way.

While job changes and losses are hard for everyone, it's important to pause and remember that you also still bring experiences, skills, characteristics, and abilities that will make this change successful and supportive. You have already had success with multiple changes at different points in your professional and personal life. You may have already experienced previous job eliminations, as a leader or an employee, and you learned from successes and mistakes.

As we saw in Chapter 4, choosing a more empowering perspective—one that isn't grounded in fear, sadness, or anxiety—will help you lead more effectively. Here are some examples of empowering perspectives:

- "I accept that I am not going to be able to make people feel good about this type of change. Whether they will be losing their job or whether it will be a colleague's job that is eliminated, this change will be painful in the short term. My goal is to treat people with compassion and respect by allowing the expression of any emotion. **I can tolerate my discomfort as others express sadness, fear, and anger, focusing on giving them the time they need and listening to how they are feeling.**"
- "I can support exiting team members by reminding them of their strengths, including sharing what I have appreciated most about working with them. I can also encourage the remaining team members to share their thoughts and feelings with exiting team members if and when appropriate. **While the current situation is difficult, we can celebrate their achievements and wish them success as they prepare for the next job.**"
- "I won't be able to guarantee that there will never be additional job losses in the future. As market conditions change, organizations need to adjust. **What I can guarantee to my remaining team members is my commitment to helping us be our best by providing clarity on our priorities and asking each team member what they need from me to succeed.** We will get through this together."
- Other: Write down any other thoughts that will help you feel strong in this situation.

Before you talk to your team about the upcoming change, take a minute to write down at least one leadership, communication, or technical strength you have—or a strength your team has all together—that you can use now. You can use the "Identify Strengths" section of the Forward Change Leadership Tool in Chapter 10.

For example, "My team members trust me, which will help all of us talk openly and honestly about our feelings and concerns." Or, "We already have weathered job eliminations in the past and got through them, so I can talk with the team about what helped us get through so we can repeat those things, as well as what didn't work so well so we can avoid repeating what didn't help."

Ask yourself:

- One strength I/we bring to this change is:
- Another strength that I or my team brings to this situation is:
- A past situation where we used our strengths to move through a change is:
- Strengths that we used then that really helped were:

Remember, this is not about ignoring deficits or challenges; it's about recognizing the good and using this to help people feel more optimistic, a powerful antidote to prevent you and the team from getting stuck in anxiety.

4. *Prepare for tough questions and reactions*

You are sure to face difficult questions as you introduce this change, both in your wider team conversations and in your one-on-one discussions. Prepare for those by using the O.U.R. (on board, uncertain, or resistant) Team Assessment and the guide for answering tough questions that was introduced in Chapter 5.

I'm not going to reproduce the whole thing here (let's save

some trees) because the questions and principles all apply to job losses just as they would to other changes. Here, I want to go a level deeper by specifically addressing *the* tough question in this situation:

"Am I going to lose my job?"

I've worked with many different leaders in many different industries, and whenever they are leading through a tough change, "Am I going to lose my job?" is at the top of their "questions I dread" list. And they're not alone. Not too long ago, when I was leading a team before starting my own business, a team member I'll call Carrie asked me this question during our weekly meeting. After 15 years of change leadership experience, I felt more equipped to handle the question, though my heart definitely picked up speed (hello, fight-or-flight reaction!).

The company was going through a tremendous amount of change and, as a result, was reducing overall head count, which prompted Carrie's question. With the increased speed and rate of change, plus ongoing advances in technology, your team, like so many others, will feel periods of uncertainty about their jobs and futures. Asking some form of "Is my job safe?" is a reasonable and not inherently problematic question for them to raise.

So what makes this question a challenging one to answer?

If the answer is yes, the person asking is going to lose their job, then, of course, it's painful to deliver that news, not to mention stressful. Some part of our "leader brain" starts rummaging through advice picked up during past HR and legal training—you know, the ones that left us feeling that one wrong word could get us or our companies sued.

Even if the answer isn't yes and the questioner's job is safe at the moment, the most accurate answer is probably something like "not at this time" or "maybe, sometime in the future." After all, there are no guarantees of job security (especially in the US, but this is becoming reality in other parts of the world too). While we may "intellectually" get that there are no guarantees when it comes to the future of our jobs, this knowledge doesn't relieve the fear and uncertainty we experience in the present, and sharing or reminding others about this truth is difficult. It's even harder if someone asks you this question before you're allowed to provide an answer. The best thing to do in that situation is to take a deep breath and say something like, "I appreciate your question, and I know not having an answer is stressful. As soon as I can, I will let you (and the team) know."

For any answer other than yes, consider using the dreaded "Will I lose my job?" question as a conversation starter.

Practice Compassion by asking questions to figure out what's going on for the person who's asking. If you can learn more about what your team member is thinking and feeling, you'll have a better chance of responding in a way that helps.

In other words, forget about giving them an answer right away, and instead give them your attention and support.

Using this approach, here's how my conversation went with Carrie (who, by the way, was not losing her job):

ME: That's a reasonable question given what's going on. I think I understand why you're asking it, but I'd like to hear more. What's causing you to ask this question right now?

CARRIE: Well, I am just feeling pretty nervous with all the changes going on. I know I was the last one hired on this team, and I've worked at companies where "last in" means "first out."

ME: (At this point, I could have jumped in but decided to get more information.) Got it. Is there anything else adding to your nervousness right now?

CARRIE: I just really like the work I'm doing...plus, things are uncertain for my partner right now too. I just wish I had more answers.

ME: Okay, that makes sense. Yeah, I wish I could give you a clear answer about what's going to happen, but you and I both know I can't. At this moment, I know of no specific plans to eliminate your job. If that should ever be the case, I would let you know as soon as I was able, and then I'd support you in finding a new job inside or outside the company. I think you are very talented, and I feel lucky to have you on my team. How about we focus on what we can do that might help?

CARRIE: Thanks. Okay, let's do that.

From there I continued to explore with her, using the 3 Priorities (Compassion, Communication, and Clarity) in a targeted way:

- I asked questions to help her identify what else she was finding stressful, then pivoted to what she's doing to help manage her stress, asking what else has worked in the past and what hasn't. She needed to hear that her feelings were normal under the circumstances, which helped reduce her anxiety because she didn't have to be stressed about *feeling stress*.
- I then asked what she loves doing, including at work. What tasks and activities give her energy and motivation? Then, I shared specific examples of the strengths I saw her bringing to her work and how she supported our team. This is practicing "scanning for the good," which, as we've discussed, reduces anxiety when our brains have been overloaded with bad news.
- Lastly, we talked about her current projects, the progress she was making, and where I could offer additional help. I also recommitted to continuing frequent check-ins with her and the team to communicate any broader changes as transparently and quickly as I could. With so much uncertainty, she needed structure and clarity where possible, which I could offer in the form of how we would work together through the changes versus coming up with predictions about the future.

5. *Envision success*

Even though it may be hard to see a successful outcome from this type of change, having a vision of what success looks like for yourself and your team as a result of this change can give you something to aim for. Consider what might be better in a week, month, or longer out. In this case, "better" may not equate to a higher level of happiness.

Imagine you've been successful in leading your team through this tough change:

- If you need to tell someone that their job has been eliminated, what makes this a successful conversation? Are you providing them with a safe space to express their emotions? Is the space private? Did you express how much you appreciate and value what they have contributed? Do they have specific details on timing or next steps, including any support being offered, to reduce some immediate uncertainty?
- Fast-forward several weeks. What obstacles have you and the team overcome? What is your team saying that you did that helped them get through this change?
- Fast-forward months from now. What benefits have been achieved for you, the team, your organization, clients, and any other stakeholders? What are they feeling, expressing, or experiencing? Are there other challenges that have surfaced that you and the team are now aware of that can be addressed?
- What are you feeling as you imagine success? Relief? Gratitude? Satisfaction? Physically feel these in your body and heart area as fully as you can. Let the thought create the experience, which is what primes your brain for this possibility to become a reality.

Remind yourself of what you can bring to this situation versus what you lack. You can lessen feelings of fear or shame for those losing their jobs by engaging thoughtfully, listening, and reminding them of their value and strengths.

6. *Create your message*

We've explored the importance and the process of creating a brief, no-more-than-one-page change message for your team in Chapter 5. Your message about the upcoming job losses should follow that same pattern and answer the same questions:

1. What's changing?
2. Why is it changing now, and what happens if it doesn't change?
3. What will the change mean to me/us, and what needs to be done differently?
4. What benefits will I/we get from supporting this change?

In situations involving job losses, though, be prepared to spend more time talking with your team about *why* the change is happening now and what the change will mean for you and the team.

Your organization might already have a communication plan and message points. If so, use them and add any additional information that is more relevant for your focus area and team. While your organization may provide the words, it's you who has the ability to deliver the message with Compassion.

7. *Have a team conversation*

When you're ready to talk with your team about the change, schedule an initial team conversation. Depending on the extent of job changes and losses, as well as your organization's communication strategy, individual conversations will probably precede a team conversation, and that's appropriate. The greater the difficulty of the change, and the more personal impact the change has on individual team members, the more conversations you'll probably need to have. Again, this is where it's important to coordinate with your manager and HR partner for guidance.

When it's time to bring everyone together, your conversation can follow the same general outline we saw in Chapter 5, with the five-part agenda:

1. Welcome and review agenda
2. Introduce the change
3. Invite the team's perspective
4. Discuss and agree on a communication plan
5. Gain commitment and review next steps

Of course, you will need to adjust what you say depending on your specific change, but here are some general tips to help you get started:

- When you introduce the change, spend extra time on what happened and why, which will give the team a bigger picture perspective. For instance: "There was a need to accelerate transformation efforts underway." Or "We needed to refocus to meet our goals for..." Or "To drive greater efficiencies."
- Restate your organization's vision for the future: "Here's where we are going... And while this is hard for all of us right now, I am optimistic and here's why..."
- Be very clear about what it means for the team: "I'll be meeting with you all individually to provide further clarification, but for now, here's where we are at..."
- Ask lots of questions, like: "What concerns you? What is

unclear?" Make sure you pause to really listen to what they're saying and capture the questions for deeper reflection later, before jumping in to answer.

- Listen to the team's feedback and make sure they know that what they share with you—even if it is critical or seems negative—is important information to know.
- Build a team communication plan together. Ask them about their communication needs, including if they'd like more communication than you are already having.

Remember, there's really no emotional reaction that can't be handled. It's just a question of how to handle them. You may need to use the moment to just listen and gather information. You can paraphrase (repeat back) what you are hearing the person say and express compassion: "I hear that you are angry about these job losses, and your reaction makes sense." Don't be afraid to let people vent. You don't need to fix something or be defensive, just listen.

8. *Follow up*

After the change has been launched, communication is vital to keeping everyone on board and on the same page. **Do quick 20-minute huddles at the start or end of the day**. Give your team the forum to share where they are having difficulty or what is working. The bigger the change (or in this case, the more extensive the job cuts), the more important it is to do this frequently, especially if the change is new or more difficult.

Continue individual conversations. After you've announced this change, continue to follow up, one-on-one and as a group, as much as possible. These are important conversations that help give confidence to remaining employees and alert you to any warning signs that indicate a remaining team member needs more support or direction. This includes meeting both with those who are exiting the organization and those who will remain.

For remaining team members, **provide additional clarity and connect them to strengths**. Ask:

- How are you feeling about the recent changes?
- As you think about your current work, is anything impacted by this change?
- What work are you enjoying the most right now? What do you feel good about accomplishing?
- Given this situation, is there any support or input you need from me that is different or that you aren't currently receiving?

For those exiting, being laid off is most likely not caused by something they did or didn't do, but they still may feel some embarrassment or shame. Continuing to talk with them, providing support, and reminding them of their strengths will help them transition. Meanwhile, team members who remain are likely to have mixed feelings to work through. There's relief that they still have a job, perhaps some guilt that they have a job when others don't, and likely anxiety about the security of their job. Add to that the "change stress" of possibly taking on additional responsibilities or adjusting to a changed workflow. All of these are normal reactions, so bring these specific feelings up in your conversations so you know where your team members stand.

If this change situation was a surprise, or if you have another change that has come up without advance warning, then Chapter 7 will help you, where the focus is on leading through a sudden change or crisis.

Chapter 7

When Change Happens Before You're Ready

What we'll cover:

- Forward Change Leadership Playbook for Sudden Changes
    - Understand the impact of the change
    - Choose your perspective
    - Quick team check-in
    - Gather additional information
    - Assess yourself
    - Identify strengths
    - Prepare for tough questions and reactions
    - Follow up

"All of these playbook actions sound great," I can imagine you thinking, "but what if I don't have any advance notice about a change and just have to deal with it?"

If this is your tough situation, or you have been in this situation before, it doesn't feel great. The sudden change is an all-too-common situation that puts leaders on the spot to respond immediately, before they can reflect, prepare, and gather the information to confidently answer their team's questions.

It happens for a variety of reasons. Sometimes there's an organizational communication breakdown, and those driving the change fail to tell their leaders about the change in advance. Yes, it's a bummer when it happens, and hopefully, there will be an opportunity in your situation to provide some thoughtfully delivered and constructive feedback so that you (and your fellow leaders) can have a better experience next time.

Another possibility here is that the change was so sudden

that it blindsided everyone. Unforeseen internal or external events can make advanced communication nearly impossible. Again, if you were leading a team through the tumultuous and unprecedented global events that began in 2020, you know what I mean!

Whatever has created your specific, unexpected situation, your job as a team leader starts with creating calm and a sense of safety for your team, and that means getting everyone together as quickly as possible, even if you don't have a detailed overview or comprehensive change message. Those are still important, but in this case, they'll need to come later.

The playbook outline below summarizes what I've seen as an effective way to lead through a surprising or unexpected change. Ideally, it gives you time—even if it's just 15 minutes—to consider what's happening and gather your thoughts in steps 1 and 2. Situations aren't always ideal, though, and you may find you need to jump straight to bringing your team together for a conversation (step 3). As time progresses, try to work through all of the steps of the change leadership process as much as you can, even if it's in a different order.

Forward Change Leadership Playbook for Sudden Changes

1. *Understand the impact of the change*

Before you gather the team together, pause to identify what, specifically, makes this situation difficult for you and your team. Focus on the change itself and not the way it was delivered to you, if possible.

Depending on the sudden change, what makes the situation difficult for you may or may not be the same as what makes the situation difficult for your team. Practice Compassion here to consider not just how shocked your team will be, but how this new change will impact them, especially in the context of anything else already happening.

If possible, take a few minutes to write down your answers in step 1 of the Forward Change Leadership Tool found in Chapter 10, or in your own note-taking system.

- One thing that will be challenging for me in leading through this change is:
- Another challenge for me or my team will be:
- Implementing this change will mean my team will need to start, stop, or continue which activities or tasks?
- Do any aspects of how we work together or communicate need to change, even if only in the short term?
- What processes, workflows, or technology must be reconfigured as a result of the change?
- Will my team need to learn any new skills to be successful in the future?
- How does this change intersect with, or influence, existing changes underway?

When you gather the team for your first conversation, ask for their thoughts on this question as well. It's a good way to let people be real with each other and share what's on their minds, which will help the team feel more connected when going through a sudden event or crisis.

2. *Choose your perspective*

You may be feeling blindsided or upset by the suddenness of what's happening. Before you meet with your team, take a couple of minutes to shift your mindset, which we looked at in detail in Chapter 4, and create a more empowering perspective about what you can do now. You may not have time to work through all your reactions before you talk with your team again, and that's okay. But even a quick check-in with yourself will set you up for a better conversation with your team.

Here are a few examples to help you get started:

- "Even though I didn't have time to prepare, I can bring my team together and create a safe space for us to share our reactions, gather questions, and reinforce our strengths. We have weathered unexpected changes in the past—both individually and as a team—and together we will also work through this one too."
- "I won't have all the answers and don't need to. My first goal is to listen to my team's reactions, concerns, and questions and share some of my own if it feels right. I can thank the team for sharing what's on their mind, address what I can, then communicate what I'll do next, including getting back to them with additional information when I have it."
- Other: write down any other thoughts that will help you feel strong in this situation.

3. *Quick team check-in*

If the change has already been announced or the rumors are already spreading, get your team together ASAP, especially if the change is a tough one. This isn't the time to compare calendars and send invitations. Get everyone you can right away, and follow up with those who can't make it as soon as you can. Call it a huddle, meeting, stand-up, or whatever language fits your culture, and make it clear that the purpose is to share some important information or to follow up on the change announcement. Remember, you don't have to prevent or fix anyone's reaction.

For now, your priorities should include:

- Getting your team together to align on what everyone has heard and understands, including sorting through facts versus assumptions if there was an organization-wide announcement.
- Providing a safe space to hear and share reactions, plus to air any initial concerns, ask questions, or address specific points where there is a lack of clarity.
- Agree on next steps, including how the team will communicate in the short term, your plan to get additional information, and how you'll communicate back, including saying "That's a great question, but I don't have that answer yet."

You may find yourself with the specific challenge of walking a line between encouraging people to be authentic with their feelings and not letting the meeting devolve into a group rant. Here's a barometer to watch for: notice when the same information starts to get repeated by different people. On the one hand, team members may actually need to put their feelings into words as a way to make sense of what's happening and to use common emotions to connect with one another. On the other, if there is no new information being gathered, then you can look to wrap up the meeting. It is okay for people to share shock, anger, sadness, and confusion, but the conversation will need to offer more than an opportunity to vent. Your team needs your leadership at this time more than ever, which means:

- Being honest about the facts as you have them now. Don't sugarcoat the situation or go down the rabbit hole of speculation. (Clarity)
  - Say: "I know we are trying to fill in the blanks because we don't have a lot of information right now. Let's focus our time and energy on what we do know and go from there."

- Imagining you are in their shoes. Think about what would help you in this situation or what you'd like to hear. (Compassion)
  - Say: "I know this is hard. I feel it too. I also know we have gone through tough changes and surprises in the past and come out strong, sometimes even better, and we'll work through this together too."
- Committing to meet daily with team members one-and-one or as a whole for a period of time, depending on the severity of the change, to reduce uncertainty and keep people focused. (Communication)
  - Say: "We'll continue to communicate frequently as we work through this, particularly at the beginning, to make sure we share information, questions, and answers that will help everyone."

Agenda:

1. Thank the team for coming together at short notice. If anyone is missing, acknowledge this and determine who will talk with that team member (if you are not able to) to bring them up to speed.
2. Launch the discussion with "I realize the announcement about…was a surprise for us all."
3. Depending on the severity of the change, you may want to also add: "I know I'm feeling concerned/upset/uncomfortable/anxious about this change, and I am sure you all are too. We'll have time to share how we feel in a moment, but first, I want to clarify what we've all actually heard in order to confirm that we are on the same page. Here's what I understand…"
4. Then ask the team, "What did you all hear?" After listening, ask, "Did anyone hear/understand something different?" Keep track of any discrepancies.

5. Invite emotional reactions, though these may have already started to come up as people have spoken. If you think it will make things easier, offer to go first. "Here's how I am feeling... Anyone feeling something similar?"
6. Continue the discussion by asking, "What else is going through your heads?" and "What questions or concerns are coming up?"
7. Lead the team toward wrapping up: "Thanks for sharing. I have a list of questions here, including some of my own...(share the list). Is there anything else for right now? I will get the answers I can and then get us back together ASAP." Give them a time frame or get something on the calendar. "In the meantime, let's remember that we have been through surprises in the past and have succeeded, and we'll make it through this challenge as well."

4. *Gather additional information*

After your check-in meeting, gather any additional information needed, using multiple sources of information or support. Your colleagues, manager, change sponsors, and HR partner are usually good places to start. Be sure to pay attention to what you hear, and ensure your team and you are dealing with facts as opposed to speculation. Especially if the change has just been announced, specific details may be limited.

If the change is not a result of a sudden crisis but because of poor internal communication, the questions below will help you get additional information from your manager or other change sponsor, which you can then communicate back to your team:

- Here is what I understand is changing... Is that correct?
- Why are we making this change now, and what happens if we don't change?

- What will the change mean to my team?
- What benefits are we hoping to get from this change? What does success look like?
- What can I or we do to support this change? Are there specific things we need to do differently right now?
- Is there anything else you can share that will be helpful for my team to know?

You may not get all the answers that you want or need, so if a question from your team remains unanswered, ask the person you are speaking with how and when to follow up so you can get an answer back to your team.

5. *Assess yourself*

Now that you've gathered more information about the specifics of this change, revisit your own feelings about the change. If this isn't a crisis but rather an organizational change that didn't get communicated in advance, try to separate out your frustration about poor change communication from the actual change itself when assessing where you fall on the O.U.R. continuum:

"I'm on board."

- While I might be a little irritated that I was blindsided, I understand why the change is being made and believe that it makes sense for my team or organization.

"I'm uncertain."

- I'm not sure I fully understand why the change is being made, and I'm unclear about whether it makes sense for my team or organization.

"I'm resistant."

- I'm not in agreement with this change right now. I think

it could be a bad idea for me, my team, our clients, and maybe the organization as a whole.

If you are feeling uncertain or resistant to the change, review Chapter 4, which will help you work through your own feelings.

6. *Identify strengths*

While this change may have been a surprise, you and your team have survived and succeeded in other challenges before. Focus on what you have going for you, not what you don't. Using step 2 in the Forward Change Leadership Tool at the end of the book, or your own note-taking system, write down at least one leadership, communication, or technical strength you have, or a strength the team has as a whole, that can be leveraged for this change:

- One strength I/we bring to this change situation is:
- Another strength I or my team brings to this situation is:
- One other strength that will support me and my team through this change is:
- Strengths that we used in the past that really helped were:

Sharing your answers with the team and letting them add their perspective is also a wonderful way to build collective optimism for the team as a whole.

7. *Prepare for tough questions and reactions*

After you have more information about this change, reassess what the impact is for your team, and then put yourself in the shoes of each team member and think about the impact on them. Write down any additional questions and concerns you think your team might raise now or as the change progresses.

If you've already spoken with your team and have a clear sense of how they feel and the questions they have, you probably don't need to spend a lot of time here. If you do want to do more preparation, see Chapter 5 for a complete overview of what to anticipate and how to respond to difficult questions.

When it comes to situations like this, any question could be a tough one. With any tough question that you can't answer in the moment, consider these tips:

- Acknowledge the question as valid. "That's a good question." Or "Yes, that question makes a lot of sense."
- Repeat the question back to the person who asked it, or ask clarifying questions to make sure you catch any confusion, since questions can come out convoluted if emotions are running high.
- Admit when you don't know the answer, but do provide any information you have.
- Promise you will find the answer and come back to the team member, and invite them to please follow up.
- Ask how not having the answer right now might get in the way and discuss how to best support the team in the meantime. This is important in order to sort out whether the team can live with the discomfort of not knowing for the time being or if not having an answer will be an obstacle to getting work done.

8. *Follow up*

After you've gathered the additional information and had a chance to consider how it will affect you, regroup with your team to answer as many of their questions as possible and share with them the information you've learned. If possible, structure this like a comprehensive change conversation, as outlined in Chapter 5, to create a full picture of the change and what it means.

If this is a big change, continue to meet with team members one-on-one and all together, at least until there is more clarity. This will help reduce uncertainty and provide some structure to help the team focus on their current work without becoming derailed by anxiety.

In Part II, we've covered the basic playbook to help you prepare to talk with your team about a change and modified some of the steps for more difficult situations. In Part III, we'll cover what happens after you've announced the change and it's underway. In particular, we'll talk about how to evaluate progress; how to approach the team if you are not seeing the behaviors, actions, and indicators that tell you the change is going in the right direction; and how to help your team remain resilient as the change continues to move forward.

Part III
The Change Is Underway

At a certain point in every change, as a leader, you'll need to shift past the place where you are announcing and preparing for the change and start leading *through* the change while it's underway. Leading your team into a change is hard, of course, but leading them through a change will have its own ups and downs, some of which will be in your control and some of which won't.

If you're reading this book while you're in the middle of some kind of organizational change, whether it's been a couple of weeks, months, or longer, how's it going?

That's not always an easy question to answer. In a lot of cases, it's obvious if you're leading through a change that is moving ahead full steam or if it's run into resistance and stalled. But there are plenty of places in between. Maybe you are confident your team is on board with the change, but you're not seeing progress. Or you and your team have been hitting the milestones, but there's tension in the air, and it still doesn't feel like everyone is fully engaged or sees the benefits of their hard work. Maybe the change itself has changed, and it's just hard to tell what progress actually means at this stage.

If you have indicators that tell you things are going well, then it's time to celebrate those successes. Feel free to skip ahead to Chapter 9 for more on that. Recognizing large or small wins along the way will help your team members keep making efforts to move the change forward, even when it gets challenging, and you'll get more of the behaviors and results you want.

What about if you're not sure if things are on track, or you are pretty clear that there is a problem? Organizational change, as we've discussed, is complicated and can have many moving parts. Hitting a snag or encountering new challenges along the way is pretty normal, but how will you know the difference between normal discomfort and derailing pain? How will you know if things are going well overall? How will you move past resistance when it shows up? The resources and ideas in Chapter 8 can help. Read on and I'll give you support at this phase of leading through change.

Chapter 8

Evaluating Progress: On Track or Not?

What we'll cover:

- Tracking change progress and adoption
  - 3 Priorities Mini Survey
  - Conducting an after-action review *during* the action
- Dealing with resistance: a deeper dive
  - Exploring different types of loss
  - Turnaround conversation

Bai worked in the government sector and had to implement a tough change—increasing the cost employees would pay for their benefits by almost 50 percent. About a month after he first announced the change, he told me, "It isn't going well. No one is happy."

I noticed right away that his response was based on the thinking that:

People are happy = Change going well

People are unhappy = Change not going well

This is a common misunderstanding when determining change progress.

Bai, I knew, had done everything as best he could, given this type of change:

- He created clarity on what was changing and why.
- He communicated what was going to happen early and kept communicating as the change launched, listening to how people were experiencing the change and adjusting what he could, based on their feedback.
- He gave employees the information they needed to adapt in the future state.

- He met the deadlines and milestones for getting it done.

From the perspective of change leadership, Bai's change was successful even if no one was happy, but this was bothering him.

As we have seen, it's important to pay attention to emotions. That said, emotions can muddy the waters when it comes to evaluating progress, especially if you don't know how to interpret what you're seeing.

It is perfectly normal for employees to feel a sense of sadness, anger, or frustration during a change. Strong emotions alone are not an indicator that a change has failed, although they can be an early warning sign that things aren't going as smoothly as you might want them to.

In Bai's situation, we discussed ways he could acknowledge and track employee sentiment to better understand the reactions he was seeing. I also helped Bai figure out what to do with the emotions he was observing. Specifically, we established a way to consistently share the emotional feedback with Bai's manager so that the organization could take additional action if needed. And perhaps most importantly, Bai and I explored how he could recognize and respond to negative emotions with Compassion, while also shifting his own perspective about how to think about success and measure progress.

Tracking Progress and Adoption of the Change

When it comes to understanding how a change is going, there are two different, but equally important, perspectives for you to consider:

1. *How well the change itself is going.* This includes key performance indicators, milestones, and metrics, which are used to measure the results of your team's actions and behaviors. Some of these will most likely be provided by your organization or from those initiating

and sponsoring the change.

2. *How well your team is adopting the change.* This includes team sentiment (how they are feeling) and also engagement (their actions and behaviors).

The first indicator, measuring actual results, seems like the easiest and most obvious answer to the "how's it going" question. The challenge, however, is that achieving metrics or KPIs (key performance indicators) may take a while to see, especially if the change you're leading takes place over an extended period of time. Outcome-based results like these are called *lagging indicators* because they only record what has already happened. So while you and your team are plugging away, waiting for the "lag" measurements to show up, it's normal to put more weight on what's right in front of you—the team's sentiment and behavior. These are examples of *leading indicators,* which give you information in real time.

Whatever indicators of success you use, it's important to agree up front with your entire team how you will all know whether the change is on track or not, including the quantitative and qualitative measures. With leading indicators, you can all adjust behaviors or practices while the change is in flight, based on what you observe happening around you.

Leading and lagging indicators are helpful only if you define them early, share them with your team, and then collectively track them on a regular basis.

This means discussing and agreeing, as a team, how to answer the following questions:

- How will we know that we are making progress and the change is on track?
- What will we be seeing, hearing, and feeling?
- What won't we be seeing, hearing, or feeling?

And then being as specific as possible on:

- Do we need to learn a new process or skill to accomplish any of these?
- What obstacles can we identify now, including existing habits, so we won't be surprised when they come up?
- What will we do when we see or encounter an obstacle?
- What will we do if we observe someone behaving in a way that is not in alignment with the new actions or behaviors?

These questions should be a key component of the earliest conversations you have as a team. In some cases, the change comes with a clear set of behaviors and actions that are needed, while in others you will need to work out with your team specifically how what they do (or don't do) will tie into the overall success of the change. This is all part of offering Clarity.

Once the change is underway, as the leader, you can reinforce your agreement about what each team member needs to do differently as a result of the change and how each person's performance will be measured in the new way of working (the specific deliverables or outcomes for which they will be held accountable). Having team input and agreement on these things as early as possible makes talking about them later, when things might be more challenging, much less awkward. You'll have more room to simply say, "So remember when we talked about X a couple of months back? I think this is one of those moments when I am not seeing (or am seeing) indicators that tell me something is off track."

But before we get too far into a discussion about what to do if things go off track, let's pause here and look at a couple of effective ways to gather and use team feedback on those emotional leading indicators in a way that is helpful, because understanding how things are going from your employees' perspectives matters more than your perspective (sorry), especially if they're the ones who have to do something differently for the change to work.

3 Priorities Mini Survey

I created the 3 Priorities Mini Survey to help you ask better questions as a change progresses. The data you'll receive will be a lagging indicator because it gives feedback on the success of your change leadership efforts and actions to date, as well as a leading indicator because it provides a real-time snapshot of how the team is responding to the change, helping you make adjustments as you continue forward. I've used this with leaders of both small and large teams to gather timely input on how their changes are going. These are Likert survey questions, so while they don't end with a question mark, you often see these types of questions (statements) in surveys used to gauge employee opinions and feelings.

Survey Questions:

1. I understand why we are changing, including what may happen if we don't make this change. (Priority = Communication)
2. I have opportunities to ask questions and share what concerns me. (Priority = Communication and Compassion)
3. I have the information, support, and resources I need to succeed. (Priority = Compassion)
4. I understand what I need to do differently on a day-to-day basis as a result of this change. (Priority = Clarity)
5. I am confident that this change will be successful. (Priority = Clarity)
6. If your change has been underway for at least 3 months, consider adding this optional question: I am satisfied

with the progress we are making on this change. (Priority = Clarity)

Directions:

1. Tell your team in advance that you would like to get their feedback to learn what is going well with a specific change and what you, as the change leader, may need to adjust to be more effective.
   - Share that you'll be sending a mini five-question survey (feel free to share the questions you'll be asking) to get their input. Let them know that the survey is anonymous, and commit to sharing the results with the team. This is *really* important. You may not be as willing to share once you see what the team says, but for the sake of transparency, it's critical that you share whatever you receive, positive or not. Remember, these are their results as well as yours, and all of you have a part to play in continuing to do things that work or making changes to get better results.
   - In order for anonymity to work, it is best to have at least three people on your team. If you have fewer than three team members, consider partnering up with a peer going through the same change, and send it to both teams.

2. Create a survey using an online service like SurveyMonkey, or whichever tool works best for you. You will get better data if people know and trust that their responses will be processed through an external source and that there will not be any negative repercussions for honest feedback.
   - Build your survey using a Likert three- or five-point

agreement scale, based on either three response options (agree, not sure, disagree) or five (strongly agree, agree, not sure, disagree, strongly disagree).
- Be very clear about which change you are asking them to respond to by naming the change initiative at the top of the survey. This is especially important if there is more than one change underway.
- Reiterate in the survey that responses will be anonymous and that you will share and discuss the results with the team.
- You can also include an optional comments text box for additional input. This might just be an open-ended space for additional information they wish to share, or you could pose a question or two, like "What else would you like to share?" or "What's one thing I or the team have done that has helped you/us be effective during this change?" or "What's one thing that I or the team could do that would help you/us be more effective going forward?"

3. Send the survey, and let people know the due date. Since the survey is short, giving them 3 to 5 days to respond should be fine. Send reminders as needed.

4. When you are ready to review the feedback, share a copy of the results with your team in advance and then schedule a meeting, giving them time to review the responses prior to the discussion.
   - When you all come together, let the team respond to the feedback first.
   - Discuss where there is agreement and what is working well. What actions have helped the team be engaged and effective in making the change?
   - If there is less-than-positive feedback, ask for

suggestions to be more effective, and agree on what these are. Make sure any suggestions pass what I like to call the "video camera test," which means that what's being described could be seen "in action" if it was recorded. If a suggestion is too vague, keep asking, "What would that look like?" For example, if someone suggests "better communication," explore together what that better communication looks like in practice for them. This is important because if you ask five people what "better communication" looks like, you'll get five different answers. One might say, "Every Friday we'll meet for 15 minutes and discuss...," while another says, "It would mean daily email updates so that there's never lag time between what you know and what I know." The more specific you can get, the greater your chance of success will be.

- Agree on specific next steps, who will take those actions and by when, and then review what success would look, feel, and sound like if the proposed actions work.
- One more tip: if *you* engage in one of the agreed upon behaviors or actions suggested, let your team actually know when you are practicing this action in real time: "You all suggested that I..., and I am practicing this now by doing..." Research suggests that you need to call out your behavioral adjustments to those who suggested them so that they recognize your efforts. This also enables you and the team to make additional adjustments on the fly.

5. It is best to complete and review this survey at least twice so you can see if there is progress over time and identify areas that need more focus. Gather team

feedback periodically (every 2 to 4 months), depending on the type and severity of the change.

You may be surprised by what you hear, but it's important to listen with respect and have an open mind, even if you don't see it in the same way. Their experience is *their experience.*

Conducting an After-Action Review *During* the Action

Another practice you can use to help you and the team track progress is an after-action review. If you've never been part of an AAR, there is a ton written on how to do this, easily found on the internet, so I'll focus on the basics here.

The concept of the AAR originally came from the US Army as a way to quickly learn from mistakes, as well as successes, while an operation was in flight rather than waiting until the end to review what happened. It was hugely helpful, and the business community adopted their own version.

Having an AAR conversation helps you and your team create greater Clarity about what has been going well and what hasn't gone as expected and then using your learnings to close the gap between those two different outcomes going forward. It's best to have this conversation after your team has had time to implement the change, which could be a week to several months depending on your situation. This information can become a guide to better behaviors, practices, and actions going forward.

One other thing to mention here, which we'll talk about further in the next chapter, is that as change gets underway, processes, actions, and even metrics can naturally shift. That's normal, but if left unacknowledged, those shifts can sometimes be used as fuel for resistance, especially if there are still team members who are not on board. In addition to discussing these shifts in regular individual and team conversations, the AAR is a great time to acknowledge these more formally.

An effective AAR answers five basic questions:

1. What did we want to happen?
2. What actually happened?
3. What went well and why?
4. What didn't go well and why?
5. What should be changed, and how, as we move forward?

AAR directions:

1. Let your team know you want to have an AAR, sharing what it is and why you'd like to have the discussion now. This is also a good time to let the team know that going forward, they can initiate an AAR conversation, especially right after an important event or milestone like overcoming an obstacle, if they believe that the rest of the team (and maybe others outside your team) would benefit from lessons learned.
2. Schedule at least 60 minutes for the first session, though in the future, you can do it in 20 minutes or 2 hours.
3. To get better participation during the meeting, send out the five questions in advance so participants have time to think about their answers.
4. You should lead the first AAR conversation but then have team members lead subsequent discussions. Be clear on what you will do with the information you gather, including how it will be shared with those outside the team. You can share key learnings without attaching names.
5. Start the conversation off by sharing the purpose and making it clear that you want to set an atmosphere of openness.
    - "The goal of this conversation is to learn from our efforts so far to help us as we go forward."

- "We are not 'grading' success or failure but highlighting opportunities to improve and successes to celebrate and repeat."
- Team members should share experiences about what actually happened (objective data) without assuming anyone's intention or blaming others.
- If needed, ask if the team wants to have some ground rules or expectations for the session, like: "It is important for everyone to participate; everyone's views have equal value. There are no right or wrong perspectives. Feel free to be creative in proposing solutions to barriers, and we'll all be open to hearing them."

6. Ask the first AAR question: "What did we want to happen?" Then continue with the others.
   - Try not to make or express judgment about what is said. Your job is to just ask for the information.
   - If people start repeating the same information, point that out, summarize what has been said, and move on to the next question or focus area.
   - A good way to kick off the third and fourth questions is to ask what *one thing* the participants thought had the greatest impact on success or mistakes so far, then go from there.
   - When trying to identify the root cause for a problem or something that didn't go well, ask "why?" several times before moving on. Again, remind people you are not assigning blame, just trying to learn.
   - It's okay to let the team express their views, but encourage them not to get stuck in what went wrong. Instead, ask, "What would you do differently next time?"

7. To close the AAR conversation, summarize any key points identified, and ask the team to share one thing that was valuable or that they learned.
8. Assign or ask for volunteers to take any follow-up actions, and set a time frame to review.

Dealing with Ongoing Resistance: A Deeper Dive

Taking the time to evaluate your progress is good, but it may make something uncomfortably clear: the reason you're not seeing the progress you wanted, or the behaviors from the team you needed, is because one or more team members is still resistant to what's happening. They're on the team, but they're not on board with the change.

This can be especially frustrating for you as the leader if you feel like you have already spent time and effort listening and understanding concerns and thought that box was checked. But change is a fluid thing, which we saw with Dimitri, back in Chapter 3, who was surprised mid-conversation to realize that his leadership team wasn't actually on board with the change they were about to launch. When venturing into the unknown, at some point, you'll encounter unexpected situations and outcomes that you and your team will have reactions to, which can then cause additional concerns. Welcome to change leadership!

Over the next few pages, we're going to take a deeper look at the causes of resistance, which can pop up at any point along the path of a change, and how you can help team members move through them. Specifically, this section will look at:

- Identifying and understanding resistance
- Having a conversation about what you observe with your team member to figure out what's going on
- Agreeing on how to move forward, including creating clarity on what actions or behaviors are needed

Resistance isn't futile, but it can't be a permanent state either.

Remember Aanya from Chapter 6, the leader who had to shut down a whole department? I worked with her and her team of leaders not just during the initial announcement but through the entire change. I worked closely with the employees who were still needed to help the organization transition with clients, while at the same time were trying to wrap their heads around what was happening with their department and jobs. During one group coaching session after the change was announced, a particularly upset employee—we'll call them Jesse—made it very clear that they were definitely not on board with the change. I share this example to help you understand what resistance can look and sound like and also how tough these conversations can be to manage.

I asked the group how they were feeling about the change, and Jesse responded, "This doesn't make sense. I mean, we've been doing a great job, and our clients are happy. I don't understand why this is happening!"

I fell into the trap that many leaders do. I got hooked by the words "I don't understand why," and so I started to explain (tell) why the change was happening. Of course, that didn't really work, because Jesse's *understanding* the change wasn't the issue; it was *accepting* the change.

"It just doesn't make sense," Jesse retorted when I was done talking, and it was like I hadn't said anything at all. "I've been working here for 4 years, really hard, and I just don't get why it has to end."

Ah, I finally realized, this wasn't about information. This was about emotion. Time to practice Compassion. I shifted gears and said, "Sounds like this was a really big shock. I can understand your reaction. Has anything like this happened to you before?"

"No," Jesse said. "I thought things were going well. I just don't understand what went wrong."

I continued using Compassion, empathizing with their feelings. "No wonder this is so difficult. You're working hard, doing all the right things, and then this happens…totally out of your control. This is a very tough situation and probably feels unfair. Unfortunately, things like this happen in organizations sometimes. A change is made that may be good for the company but not so good for some people like you."

I noticed heads nodding in agreement around the room, so, feeling emboldened, I continued. "Is anyone else feeling this way?"

A couple of others chimed in and started talking about the fact that it was tough. Some also added that they *did* understand the rationale for closing the department, which I hoped would resonate with Jesse. Their peers could see that this change wasn't because they had done something wrong. (Facilitation tip: it always helps if someone other than you can share how they are moving forward.)

I thought the conversation was going well. I'd found a way to connect with not only Jesse but also with many others in the room. Well done, me.

"That's right; it is unfair," Jesse jumped in again and burst my bubble. "I just don't get it. See, we all know we were doing everything right."

Crud.

We went around in circles a few more times before I said, "I need to keep going with our session now, Jesse, but let's continue talking when we're done."

At the end of the session, I tried to catch Jesse's eye, but they walked out of the room. Later, I found out that Jesse had been repeating disbelief and the "I don't understand" message for several weeks to anyone who would listen, and this behavior was negatively impacting not only Jesse and the team but clients as well.

This is a situation that many leaders would find tough to handle.

Jesse's teammates had felt the same things but now showed signs of moving forward. Jesse, on the other hand, was stuck. On one hand, they had every reason to feel angry and fearful. The change was a total surprise and not Jesse's "fault." On the other hand, the change was clearly communicated, employees were being treated with respect and provided with support, and clients still needed professional help through the transition.

Jesse's manager had been practicing Compassion, approaching Jesse's resistance with curiosity, trying to understand if there was something else contributing to it and if there was a concern that hadn't been addressed. After several conversations, however, it was clear that something else had to be done. At this point, the manager and I discussed shifting from the "uncovering concerns" conversation to the "improving performance" conversation. If Jesse wasn't able to move past resistance, we all agreed that they might have to leave the company sooner than planned.

Here's a summary of that conversation, followed by a tool to help you uncover what might be causing resistance in your own team during a change and a framework you can use if you need to have a conversation to help your team member shift direction to succeed.

LEADER: We've talked about your concerns and things that can help you in previous conversations. (They gave Jesse examples.) But I'm not seeing or hearing those new actions or behaviors from you yet, which tells me that you are not making this change. Do you know what I am talking about?

(The leader is framing the discussion they want to have and also checking in to make sure Jesse understands the situation in the same way.)

JESSE: Yes, but it's hard to move forward when I don't like or agree with what's happening.

LEADER: Yes, I get it. I have a hard time with what's happened as well, and I wish it was different. Unfortunately, your feelings are causing you to act in ways that aren't helpful. (The leader shared an example of a recent client interaction.) I understand that this is hard to hear, but I'm talking with you with the hope you can understand what you need to do differently to be successful, even if it's a tough time. Let's refocus on the outcomes we need and what you can do to achieve them.

The leader is still practicing Compassion but also creating Clarity about the impact of Jesse's feelings on their behavior, including sharing a specific example.

The leader went on to outline what actions and results were needed, asked Jesse what they could commit to, and then agreed on a timeline to review progress. Several weeks later, Jesse left for a new opportunity. While it was hard for Jesse and the leader, it was the best decision under the circumstances.

Resistance left unaddressed becomes toxic for everyone involved, including the employee themselves. This is true whether the resistance is due to something that is being lost or whether there is a concern that's more future-oriented, like a team fearing the unknown or not having a skill or the resources needed to be successful. Resistance could also be caused by more than one thing. This is why people's level of resistance could come and go as a change progresses.

If you see resistance to an in-process change from anyone in your team, the first step is to try to identify what might be causing it. That may immediately be clear, but if you want some help, I've created a loss exploration process, which you'll find in the Forward Change Leadership Tool in Chapter 10. Review the outline below, and if it's helpful to your situation, spend a few minutes filling in the chart before you talk with an employee who may be knowingly or inadvertently giving you indicators that they are not on board. You can also share the questions, or the whole chart, with your team to help them identify what might be causing resistance on their part.

Loss exploration directions:

First, think about the general type of loss that the employee may be facing or what else may be causing concern. These can be generally thought about in the following categories:

- Scope and influence (e.g., losing degrees of responsibility, power, or control)
- Expertise (e.g., losing being the go-to person)
- Accomplishment (e.g., losing a feeling of pride and purpose in the work completed up to this point because of a shift in direction, making past work feel obsolete)
- Relationships (e.g., losing a boss, peers, clients, or other valued relationships or losing being part of a team, peer, or other group)
- Routines and structure (e.g., losing the current way work gets completed)
- Work they love to do (e.g., losing activities they enjoyed, things that played to strengths and gave purpose)
- Career progression (e.g., loss of the "next step" or knowing where the job will lead and control over their career path)
- Inspiring future vision (e.g., a dream or ideal they were holding on to that helped them feel energized and engaged)

Next, think about the specific form of that loss or concern and use the middle column to write that down. For example: Toni is feeling a loss of expertise because he will "lose" being the expert using the current relationship management system and needs to learn a whole new system as a result of the change.

You have already learned about actions you can take to support your team members, so in a third column, write some things you can do to help the employee. Almost any action will begin with practicing Compassion by sharing your observations and then asking the employee for their perspective. Before agreeing on actions that would help, be sure to ask the employee what they would like to do.

If you share this process with your team, remember that your action is simply using Compassion to help them name their loss and then acknowledging this loss as understandable. Listen to what the loss is like for them, and let them tell you what they need. At first, they may need time to just vent and process their feelings before being able to tell you what they need from you to move forward.

Also, expect their needs and perception to evolve as the change progresses (i.e., they may need you just to have compassion and listen to them at first, but later they may ask for help to learn a new skill).

Turnaround Conversation

When you're ready to talk to your team member, approach the conversation with the goal of helping them adjust their behavior to switch direction, getting them on a path that will be more successful.

This kind of conversation can be difficult for a variety of reasons, including the ones bulleted below that I hear most often:

- The conversation is going to be awkward and difficult for me and probably for them too.
- I am concerned about how they will react. I don't want to deal with their defensiveness.
- Giving negative feedback (or feedback that may be perceived as negative) will harm our relationship. They might resent me.
- If I just give them more time, they'll get the message and shift their behavior on their own.
- The difficult feedback I have to give to them feels more

personal (emotional), and I'm not sure I am supposed to give that kind of feedback in a work setting.

If you are hesitating, it's a good time to practice reframing, a process we explored in detail in Chapter 4. Be clear on the specific things that are holding you back, then use a more empowering perspective to shift your mindset.

Reframing will help you go from a mindset like the ones above and help you approach the conversation with the attitude that:

- Most people do, in fact, want to do good work.
- Giving feedback is giving someone an opportunity to improve.
- Feedback is information. Without it, the individual will not be operating with all the data they need to succeed, which will hurt the whole team.
- As long as an employee is part of my team, I owe it to them to provide information about how they or their behavior is being perceived. The feedback belongs to them, especially if others are talking about them and they are unaware.

A good turnaround conversation shares the same common features:

- Begin by *framing* the purpose of the conversation and gaining agreement from your team member that they understand the focus and specific situation or behavior you want to discuss. (This is generally a good way to start any conversation, true whether you're giving feedback to help them get on the right track or celebrating great work).
- Next, ask questions to *discover* your team member's

understanding, reasoning, feelings, or perspective about the situation. When providing corrective feedback, seek your team member's perspective first before offering your assessment. Once they give their perspective, you can clarify the behavior and actions you see that need to shift or change or be celebrated.

- *Recognize* the impact of the behavior by sharing how the impact has not met expectations.
- Finally, help your team member *focus* on how they will leverage their success further or shift their behavior to improve. Ask questions to establish a good starting point and plan of action.

Use the sample conversation starters and questions below to help you have the Turnaround Conversation.

Frame:

- "I'd like to talk with you about… I want to make sure we are both clear on the outcomes we are looking for and how you can deliver on them, including how I can help."

Discover:

- "I want to share some observations with you, but first, I'd like to get your perspective on what's going on related to…"
- "Why do you think that's happening?"
- "What do you think has been preventing you from being at your best?"

Recognize:

- "Here is what I have seen/heard…and here is the impact

it's having..."
- "Here's what I see you needing to shift/change..." (Focus on *one* thing at most.)
- "Are you concerned about anything I am asking you to shift?"

Focus:

- "What do you think you can do differently?"
- "What might get in your way?"
- "What strengths can you leverage to help you? Here's what I have seen you do that can help..."
- "What's the best possible result we could achieve?"
- "What's the first step you could take and when will you start?"
- "What action can I take to help you?"

Plan a follow-up conversation no longer than 2 weeks from the time you have this discussion to adjust the plan or celebrate progress, which will reinforce positive movement forward. We'll talk more about how to use team strengths and celebrate success in Chapter 9.

Chapter 9

Creating Resilience

What we'll cover:

- Dealing with change fatigue
- Identifying and leveraging strengths to build resilience
- Celebrating successes to create team unity and better results

Given the hectic pace of change in most organizations, my conversations with clients have evolved in the last year. Where they once called me for advice about leading through a specific change, now I find that we're talking about how to lead through multiple ongoing changes—and how to do so in a way that helps them and their teams remain resilient and prepared for the inevitable changes still on the horizon.

To be clear, even the most resilient teams will get frustrated, anxious, sad, or tired at times. Resilience isn't some superhuman state that shields you from these normal human emotions. Resilience is, quite simply, a way of interacting with yourself through the intense ups and downs in the world around you. Practicing resilience means building enough awareness to recognize and name the low periods honestly, then taking a deep breath, accepting what you and the team are feeling, figuring out together how to support each other through these times, and then doing it all over again when another low appears.

Resilience comes from and is influenced by a variety of factors, including your past experiences and your genetics, neither of which you can change. Research (and probably your own experience) shows, however, that whatever your starting point, you can learn skills to build resilience, which typically means finding new ways to deal with stress when the actions you used to take aren't working so well anymore. In this chapter, we'll look at some things that can drain your energy, making you less resilient during change, and then we'll focus on what you can do to support resilience in yourself and your team. As always, it'll be up to you to lead the way and model behaviors and actions that build resilience.

Dealing with Change Fatigue

It's become common for organizations to keep expecting their people to do more with less under the guise of continuous improvement or creating efficiency. I don't disagree with the underlying intention to save money and create competitive advantage, but we've seen this often enough now to understand that it can lead to multiple under-resourced change efforts that end up creating apathy, frustration, and burnout across the workforce. In other words, change fatigue. I know a lot of people, myself included, who look in the mirror some days and see the perfect definition of change fatigue staring back at them, a look that says, "I'm already too busy to manage it all."

In fact, how often do you hear "busy" when you ask how a coworker is doing? How often do you say it yourself? These days, I hear "busy" as shorthand for:

- "I'm just plowing through to reach the goal(s)."
- "I'm tired but don't want to slow down because I might lose momentum."
- "I am nervous about *not* being busy because others would think that what I do doesn't matter that much."
- "I have a long to-do list so I don't have to think about, feel, or deal with things I would notice if I wasn't busy."

The problem isn't being busy itself. There is a place and time for being busy, and for the emotions that go along with this state, which can focus or motivate us when needed. The problem is that "busy" has become a constant state, the new normal baseline that is wearing people out. Gartner, a global research and advisory firm, did research on change fatigue and confirmed that employees' ability to absorb change reduced by 50 percent beginning in 2020 because of the pandemic and other global events we've collectively dealt with on top of our own personal and professional changes.[13]

According to their research, employees reported that it was the toll of multiple, day-to-day, small workplace changes versus the large-scale initiatives that caused them the most fatigue.

In other words, things that seem small still need to be managed well, or they can build into a much bigger issue.

The increased pace and rate of change in organizations doesn't just throw more new changes at us; it affects how often those changes end up shifting once they are underway, which also adds to the fatigue. Ashley, who was part of a group of leaders tasked with leading through a particularly complicated, multiyear transition, summed this up nicely during our group conversation, "We are changing our change, and this change will probably change again!"

Ashley brought up a great point. We saw earlier how important it is to set a clear expectation *up front* that the change you're undertaking together will naturally shift over time, especially once things get underway. These shifts are normal and not necessarily an indication that there is a problem with the change itself. Setting this expectation, and then keeping the lines of communication open and encouraging team members to share any obstacles they encounter along the way, will help to reduce frustration and the other emotions that can lead to change fatigue.

Gartner's research also affirmed that teams that measured high on trust and cohesion scales weathered change better than teams who reported lower trust and cohesion, highlighting the power of working together to make change as opposed to using only a directive, top-down approach. Of course, that lines up with what we have covered so far, especially the importance of practicing the 3 Priorities to partner through change. As we start to approach the end of this book, let's take a closer look at two easy actions that will help you and your team feel good and have fun—key ingredients for resilience.

Identifying and Leveraging Strengths to Support You and Your Team

I am a big fan of books that offer effective strategies for building workplace resilience. In one of them, *Resilience: The Science of Mastering Life's Greatest Challenges,* Dennis Charney and Steven Southwick explain that people can train their brain to be more resilient using ten research-based strategies:

1. Keeping a positive attitude
2. Reframing stressful thoughts
3. Developing a moral compass
4. Finding a resilient role model
5. Facing fears
6. Developing active coping skills
7. Establishing and nurturing a supportive social network
8. Prioritizing physical well-being
9. Training the brain
10. Playing to your strengths

Out of these things, the strategy most leaders don't leverage enough when leading change is *playing to strengths,* both their own and the strengths of their team.

I'll admit that earlier in my career I used to do some serious eye-rolling when I'd hear people talk about leveraging strengths to improve performance. I wanted to like the idea because of its inherently positive nature, but I was highly skeptical of any strategy that didn't seem "serious" enough. *Strengths* just sounded unprofessional. Today, I've done a complete one-eighty, in part because of my own positive results as a team leader and executive coach working with teams to identify and utilize their strengths, but also because of what I've learned through neuroscience (big surprise) and the accumulating body of supportive research.

My change of heart all started when my former employer, ADP, acquired The Marcus Buckingham Company. Marcus and his team are pioneers in researching and writing about the power of focusing on strengths to help individuals and teams be their best. Their work confirms that people who specifically make time during their work week to do activities they love, what Marcus calls "strengths," are happier, more resilient, and more productive. "Of the eight conditions that are the signature of the highest-performing teams, there is one in particular that stands out…as the single most powerful predictor of a team's productivity. It is…'I have the chance to use my strengths every day at work.'"[14]

One of the things that changed my perspective was that Marcus showed me how to differentiate a *strength* from a *skill*. You can be skilled at doing something, like putting a PowerPoint deck together, but it doesn't energize you like a strength would. Doing activities you love makes you feel good. Feeling good reduces anxiety and, in turn, helps you build resilience, and that is why focusing on strengths is an especially good lever to pull when leading through change.

So if this is such a great strategy, why aren't more people talking about it? What gets in the way of seeing and using strengths? For one thing, many of us were taught, through culture or family, that it is arrogant to acknowledge our strengths. This becomes clear whenever I ask someone to make a list of all the things they'd like to improve about themselves or things they consider weaknesses. Off they go, easily listing item after item. In contrast, when I then ask the same person to list all of their strengths or what they appreciate about themselves, they often stall out after about six items. Offering some prompts like "What would your pet say about you?" is always good for an additional three or so, but you get my point here. We're not naturally comfortable acknowledging strengths.

To leverage your strengths and build your resilience, though, you need to first accept that it's not only okay to focus on what gives you energy but it's scientifically proven to benefit your well-being. The next thing you need to do is identify your unique, particular strengths.

Think of activities you did at work over the last couple of weeks.

- First, recall something you enjoyed doing. Maybe it was a presentation you gave or the quiet time where you created a spreadsheet to organize your data in a better way. **How did doing that activity make you feel?**
- Next, remember something you didn't like as much. Maybe it was a presentation you had to give or forcing yourself to sit alone and complete that spreadsheet you've been putting off. **How did doing this activity make you feel?**

Whether you love or hate doing presentations or creating spreadsheets, chances are the things that you listed in response to the first question probably made you feel a lot better than those in the second list. Now you have an internal barometer for what a strength is (i.e., the activities you really enjoy).

If needed, you can refine this list further using these additional questions:

- What have you really enjoyed doing at work or on various projects?
- What projects in the past week have been most energizing for you?
- What is your perfect day at work, where you are doing what you really like most?

This same activity is a great conversation starter to have with your team. The first time I asked these questions with my team, we found out that while our team members had some similar "loves," there were also a lot of differences. One person in particular shared that she really loved the operational aspects of putting learning programs together. We collectively agreed to leverage her strength more for that, since most of us preferred the design aspects. Several other team members were able to do some task swapping when they discovered that their teammates really enjoyed doing tasks that drained them.

A word of caution on doing this activity: if team trust is not high, talking about the activities that they don't like can feel risky to some team members, especially if those activities are currently part of their job. Another option in this scenario is inviting team members to complete the activity in advance and publicly sharing only those things that they love most.

There's never a bad time to go through this process with your team. Recognizing strengths, I've come to realize, is good leadership. But it's particularly important in the midst of a change, and it's a valuable tool to revisit once a change—or perhaps more than one—is underway.

Once you have the time to understand a change and try it out for a while, you'll have a new idea about the types of activities or tasks you'll need to stop, start, or continue for that change. At that point, bring the team together for a specific discussion about strengths and how your particular change impacts them doing the activities they love most. If they can see that you're there to help them do activities they love, even if it's in a future state, they'll be more likely to engage with the change and make any behavior changes that are needed.

Partnering with your team to discover, agree, and align on what they need to do on a day-to-day basis after a change can be so much easier if everyone can see themselves in the future state, doing the things they love to do. Your job as the change leader is to continue to help them understand what they need to stop, start, or continue doing as the change progresses.

Let's look more closely at the different possibilities, starting with scenarios where team members will still be able to do activities they love.

They will still be able to do activities they love. This is a best-case scenario! In most cases, if you reach this conclusion, the change is on a good track for success. If your team member still feels uncertain or resistant to the change, even if it's playing to their strengths, ask if they understand what's happening in the same way you do. If there is resistance, it may be for another of the reasons outlined in Chapter 8.

They will still be able to do activities they love, but they'll need to do them in a new way. While continuing to use their strength can make adopting the change easier, this team member may still experience a sense of loss related to giving up how the work was done. Again, talk with them about how they see the change and what it means for them. Check to make sure they understand and agree that they'll be able to continue doing the things they love in the future state, even though *how* they do them may take some getting used to.

During your team or individual conversations about the change, after people have had time to process and have started the change process, help them connect their strengths to the new way of working by asking:

- Which of your favorite tasks or activities are you able to continue doing?
- What other strengths can you bring to help us all move forward successfully?

They may no longer be able to do some or many of the activities they love doing. Yes, this is the hardest outcome, but it doesn't have to be a complete disaster.

- First, make sure both you, as the change leader, and your team member are clear on what activities will cease.
- Next, talk about the types of activities your team member loves to do that they will still be doing after the change takes effect. Will they still spend most of their time doing things they love? If not, how many of their new activities still play to their strengths? If they're having a hard time even with that, explore which of the new activities the employee might enjoy a little, or at least not make them want to pull their hair out.
- If they won't do most of the activities they love to do, then this would be a good time to have a career conversation. Help them figure out how they want to handle the situation, including if there is a different role that would play more to their strengths.

This last situation is where things can get tricky. We all have to do some tasks or activities during the course of our day that we'd rather not be doing; that's part of working life. That said, if a person spends most of their time doing activities that drain them, it decreases engagement and increases stress. But by making time to do activities we enjoy more often, we build our resilience for the things that we enjoy less, leaving us less likely to suffer from change fatigue, which can lead to burnout.

Here's proof. In a study done by the Mayo Clinic, physicians who said they spent at least 20 percent of their time or more at work doing activities they found "professionally satisfying" had significantly lower levels of burnout than those who spent less than 20 percent doing activities that they found professionally satisfying.[15]

Can you and your team spend at least 20 percent of your time doing activities that are satisfying and fulfilling? I know you're all very busy, so you might be thinking, "Yeah right, Elizabeth.

We barely have time to do all the things we have to do, let alone make more time to do the fun things." I hear you.

Consider this, though. First, I'm not talking about doing fun stuff *all* the time (though if that describes you and your gig, nicely done). Second, if busy doctors can find a way to spend 20 percent of their time doing what they really like, even where it really can be about life and death, can you and your team find a little extra time somewhere? Remember that leveraging strengths helps people feel stronger and more optimistic, which we already learned in Chapter 2 is a powerful antidote to fear and negativity, the real culprits behind resistance to change.

Celebrating Successes for Better Results

Remember Mara, the leader I introduced in Chapter 3? She was the one who told me that people are desperate for good news. She had led her team through so many changes that she'd developed a successful communication plan that she used again and again, adjusting it only slightly for each situation, depending on the details of what needed to be implemented.

These were Mara's keys for communication that worked so well:

- She used different modes of communication, including large town hall meetings (she led a larger department), smaller team meetings with her direct reports, and individual check-ins. And yes, she'd send regular weekly and monthly email updates to supplement her other communications, but never as a stand-alone method.
- She and the other leaders who reported to her created opportunities for two-way conversations both between themselves and with their teams.
- She and her people leaders celebrated successes, which helped them build momentum. Sharing good news and celebrating successes was a key part that was *never*

dropped from Mara's plan.

Mara's Team Communication and Celebration Plan	Frequency
30-minute team and individual meetings to align on execution of goals, celebrate successes, and help remove barriers related to the change across the organization.	Weekly
Celebrating Success email to recognize and share great accomplishments as people adopt new actions and behaviors.	Weekly
Strategy sessions to review progress against the business plan and change initiatives with key stakeholders, partners, and leaders. Discuss successes and lessons learned along the way.	Quarterly
Spotlight focus areas to communicate specific activities, problems, positive results, or lessons learned.	Daily 20-minute huddles at the beginning of the major change, then the team will decide on frequency as the change continues
3 Priorities Mini Survey to capture data on how employees are experiencing the change and the management team's change leadership efforts. Results are shared and discussed so employees know their feedback was heard and has influence on how the change is managed.	Quarterly

It's a comprehensive, and consuming, communication plan. Even Mara admitted, "Yeah, it took time, but it was definitely worth it." She knew that because she and her team tracked employee feedback and sentiment through the 3 Priorities Mini Survey, their results improved with each round. Later, they decided to see if there was any correlation between these survey results and client satisfaction. Much to their delight, the answer was yes; as employee engagement improved, client satisfaction improved over the same period. While we know that a better employee experience leads to a better client experience (Service-Profit Chain, anyone?), it was good to see this play out in the data the team had collected. I can tell you from conversations I had with Mara's boss and boss's boss (who reported to the CEO), they thought it was worth it too.

If I was going to map out the connection between celebrating success and building resilience, it would look something like this:

Recognition for great work + Feeling good and optimistic about results = Building resilience

Deciding what recognition for great work and celebration looks like is up to you and your team. Some people's idea of fun may feel like work to someone else, so it's a good idea to build your celebration muscles by trying some different things and seeing what works. The goal is fun, which should happen with as much ease and joy as possible. Here are additional thoughts:

- See if there is a team member who would find coming up with celebration suggestions to present to the team to be an energizing activity and ask them to take this on.
- You may have a colleague who is especially good at this, or your organization may have an event-planning team who could make some suggestions.
- Celebration can be a multi-team event, so join with other teams to spread the joy and help build internal

networking and silo-removing opportunities.

- When it comes to recognition, ask each team member how they like to be recognized. Some will like this done in public, while some may prefer a private conversation.
- If it's a team that is working virtually or are in multiple locations, there are many ideas and options available if you do a quick online search.

GREAT JOB! 2.0 Conversation to Celebrate Success

What does a meaningful celebration conversation look like? I'm glad you asked. I call the following framework "GREAT JOB! 2.0" because it's an upgrade from the standard pat-on-the-back "great job" that too many leaders fall back on as their extent of recognition and celebration.

The outline below is probably at least a 20-minute conversation in a one-on-one setting, though you can adjust as needed. Remember to take as much time to appreciate successes, and what made those successes possible, as you would do trying to understand something that goes wrong.

If you want to recognize great work in a team setting, start by having this one-on-one conversation with the person you want to recognize, and ask while you're there if it's okay to share their contribution during the next team meeting so others can benefit. If the person is more on the introverted or shy side, they'll appreciate a heads-up prior to the group conversation. And if success meetings are new for your team or organization, some of the people in the group may feel like they are bragging. As I shared earlier, most of us have been taught that acknowledging strengths and accomplishments—or showing emotions like happiness, joy, or even having fun—is unprofessional, not synonymous with hard work, or could be taken as bragging. If you are having fun at work, then you must not be busy enough.

If you've found yourself uncomfortable giving or receiving

praise for any of these reasons, you're not alone. One research team found that most managers who participated in their study felt more comfortable expressing anger than joy at work.[16]

You and your team members can overcome these hesitations by getting more practice celebrating...not the worst thing to add to someone's to-do list. I like to say that it's not bragging if it's true, so just acknowledge any discomfort as normal. Encourage others, if they are not totally on board with this concept, to give it a try, noticing any discomfort you or they experience while you continue to practice. This will most likely be one of those times where experiencing discomfort is more a sign of pushing against an old boundary by trying something new versus a sign that something is wrong.

Conversation framework: You can use the prompts below, but please feel free to put this into your own words.

Frame: "Congratulations on a great job with... I want to take time to celebrate what you did and also how to build on your success."

Recognize: "This is a great accomplishment!" "What I really appreciate is..." "I saw your strengths come through when you..." (Give specific examples and share strengths you observed and the impact.)

Discover: "What do you think made the difference in your success?" "Where were you at your best?" "Who else contributed or collaborated with you?" "What strengths do you feel were helpful to you?"

Focus: "What do you think we can build on from this success?" "What did you learn from this win that we can preserve and repeat?" "What can other people learn from this?"

Notice how you feel during and at the end of this conversation. Is there joy, relief, or even pride in someone else's contribution? Is this a team member who is one of your top performers, or conversely, are they someone who has struggled, and so this win means that much more to them and you? Take a few minutes and really be present for these positive feelings, so your brain and body get the most benefit. You may feel more cheerful, hopeful, confident, encouraged, or relaxed. You are taking time and seeing what is good in these moments, giving your brain and body a much-needed reprieve from bad news or what's wrong.

Even if you (or your team member) can hear a faint critical voice coming through, reminding you that there is still plenty to do or fix, that's okay. Tell yourself and them that this celebration is *real*; you are celebrating what's true. There's enough difficulty, fear, and irritation to go around, so give yourself and your team members time to enjoy the full benefits of feeling good. Congratulations!

Part IV

You Take It from Here...

Now it's time for you to celebrate being at the end of this book. Go you! I know how busy you are, so I'm honored by your curiosity and dedication to take on the challenge of becoming an even stronger change leader. The final chapter is the Forward Change Leadership Tool, a quick and condensed version of the Playbook steps, which you can use now or at any future time when you are leading your team through a change.

While I would love to be able to take a walk with you and hear what has been most helpful, or what else I could add to make this book more useful, I'll settle for you taking a few minutes and answering some questions for yourself:

What's one thing you're taking away that's most relevant for you right now?

Is there an action or behavior you'd like to try out in the next couple of days with your team?

What's a strength you noticed while reading, where you thought to yourself "Yes, I'm already doing that"?

What's one thing you were skeptical about, wondering if that would actually work?

Is there something you'd like to *stop* doing as you lead through change?

I'm sure you've already thought this, but being a leader is a lot of responsibility, equal parts humbling, frustrating, satisfying, and exciting. It isn't easy to lead the way, especially when things are uncertain or difficult. This is why I hope, no matter what you will add to your to-do list today, that you'll definitely take a moment to acknowledge an accomplishment or success you've had, or even getting through a failure, as your next success will likely come from what you have learned through this experience. That's how we do it. And I will always celebrate you for trying to be the best leader you can be.

Chapter 10

Forward Change Leadership Tool

Sometimes what you need most at the start of a big change is a consolidated, action-focused checklist of the things you need to do, in the order you need to do them. That's what this tool is—an overview of the action steps that you've read about in the past nine chapters, without the explanations, scripts, and stories to distract you. This tool gives you a simpler way to run through the steps to help you get each change off to a good start.

You can refer back to previous chapters if you need more information about anything here.

Start with Yourself

Before you talk to your team, spend a few minutes understanding your own feelings and reactions to the upcoming change.

- *Am I currently on board, uncertain, or resistant to the change that's coming?* Pause to name your feelings, treating them as important data that will either help or hinder you as you make the change.

- *If I'm uncertain or resistant, why do I feel the way I do?* What are your feelings trying to tell you? What's the wisdom in your feelings?

    - Can I reframe my negative thoughts to create a more empowered perspective to help me lead through this change?

- What are the facts versus my assumptions in this situation?

- Is my perspective the only possibility?

- Is a more optimistic outcome possible?

- What strengths can I bring to manage this situation?

- When I've experienced something like this before, what did I learn that I could apply here to help me or my team?

- What have I learned from other leaders who have moved through difficulties with both realism and grace that could help me in this situation?

- What aspects of this change *can I* control?

Understand the Impact of the Change

Take a few moments and think about your path forward. Write down your answers.

- One thing that will be challenging for me in leading through this change is:

- Another challenge for me or my team will be:

- What activities or tasks will my team need to start, stop, or continue in order to implement this change?

- Do any aspects of how we work together or communicate need to change, even if only in the short term?

- What processes, workflows, or technologies must be reconfigured as a result of the change?

- Will my team need to learn any new skills to be successful in the future?

- How does this change intersect with, or influence, existing changes underway?

Identify Strengths

Use the question prompts below to identify and list experiences, skills, characteristics, or abilities that you and members of your team bring to support this change effort.

- One strength I/we bring to this change situation is:

- Another strength I or my team brings to this situation is:

- A past situation where we used our strengths to move through a change was:

- Strengths that we used then that really helped were:

Prepare for Tough Questions and Reactions

Think about the change from your team's perspective, including processes they might need to do differently, and use the tools below to help you identify activities they like that they might not get to do anymore, skills they'll need to learn, increases in their current workload, and the like.

O.U.R. (on board, uncertain, resistant) Team Assessment

Directions:

1. Write the names of each team member in the first column.
2. Consider the approaching change from each person's perspective. What could be the consequences, or the *perceived* consequences, for this specific person? Write that in the second column.
3. In the third column, write down how that person might initially feel about the change.
4. In the fourth column, consider what they might need from you to get on board with the change. This could be one of the 3 Priorities or something practical like skill development or training.
5. Lastly, given what you know right now, would you consider them to be on board, uncertain, or resistant to this change?

Team member	What might happen to this person as a result of this change?	How might they feel?	What will they need to make the change?	Initial reaction: on board, uncertain, or resistant?

Next, write down questions or concerns you expect to hear from your team:

1.

2.

3.

4.

Take a few moments to draft some things you could say in response to the questions above. If you are pretty sure there will be resistance, you can use the guidance on tough questions in Chapter 5 to help you formulate your responses.

1.

2.

3.

4.

Envision Success

Imagine you have been successful in leading your team through this change. Practice seeing and feeling success as clearly and fully as you can and responding to the questions below.

- What has been accomplished?

- What or who are you particularly proud of? (Imagine the person who might have the most resistance at the start becoming one of the most valuable contributors to success.)

- What obstacles have you overcome?

- What does your team say you did that helped them be successful? (See their smiling faces; imagine the meetings and conversations where you all are reflecting on your success together, sharing stories, laughing, and talking about all obstacles you overcame.)

- What benefits have you achieved for the team, the organization, the clients, and other stakeholders? What are they feeling, expressing, or experiencing?

- What are you feeling as you imagine your success? Relief? Happiness? Gratitude? Satisfaction? (Physically feel these in your body and heart area as fully as you can. Let the thought create the experience, which is what primes your brain for this possibility to become a reality.)

Now, come up with a one-to-three-sentence statement that captures a positive future vision of this change for your team. If you need more information about how to do this, refer to Chapter 5.

My positive future vision is:

Create Your Message

Write your answers to the following questions on a single page, forcing yourself to stick to higher-level answers. This will be the vision statement you can share with your team. (Make sure this aligns with any broader organizational messaging, and share with your manager prior to sharing with your team, if appropriate.)

The name of this change is:

- What's changing?

- Why is it changing now, and what happens if it doesn't change?

- What will the change mean to me/us, and what needs to be done differently?

  - What will be gained?

  - What will be lost?

  - What new actions, behaviors, and results are we looking for (what needs to be done differently)?

- What benefits will we get from supporting this change? (For example, there may be benefits for clients and the organization as a whole in the short or longer term, but also consider whether there are specific benefits for your team and their professional and personal development.)

Have a Team Conversation

The actual team conversation is outlined in detail, including text to include in a slide deck, in Chapter 5. Below is a checklist of questions to consider *before* having the team conversation:

1. Have you completed steps 1 through 5? (The exception is if you and your team find out about a change at the same time, then go to Chapter 7 for the guidance on the quick team check-in.)

2. Have you blocked out enough time for the first conversation, including having time available after the meeting in case some team members need to talk further with you?

3. Have you considered any logistical challenges for your unique situation? (Will everyone be at the meeting, or will you need to connect individually with anyone?) This is especially important to consider if this change involves job losses. Refer to Chapter 6 for more information on dealing with staff reductions.

4. Lastly, what would a positive conversation or outcome be or look like? (For example, see people being curious, listening and asking questions, even if they disagree. See yourself being able to handle any tough question, even if it means following up later. If you don't know how to respond, say that.)

Follow Up

Your role as a change leader doesn't end when the change is announced and launched. As time passes, here are a few tools to continue to check in and support your team. Additional helpful information about gathering team input and feedback using an after-action review and the 3 Priorities Mini Survey, identifying and utilizing strengths, measuring progress, and celebrating success can be found in Chapters 8 and 9.

Considering this change, what type of follow-up actions or conversations do you anticipate needing to do or have in the next 2 months?

1.

2.

3.

4.

Loss Exploration Tool

The loss exploration guidance referenced in Chapter 8 will help you and your team members understand and work through resistance that arises along the way, particularly if people are losing something important to them.

You can fill this chart out from your own perspective or use it as the starting point for a discussion with the whole team.

Type of Loss	Name and What They Are Losing	What Support They Need
Scope/Influence *e.g., losing degrees of responsibility, power, and control*		
Expertise *e.g., losing being the go-to person*		
Accomplishment *e.g., losing a feeling of pride and purpose in the work completed up to this point because of a shift in direction, making past work feel obsolete*		
Relationships *e.g., losing a boss, peers, clients, et al. or losing being part of a team, peer, or other group*		

Routines/Structure *e.g., losing the current way work gets completed*		
Work They Love to Do *e.g., losing activities they enjoyed, things that played to strengths and gave purpose*		
Career Progression *e.g., loss of the "next step" or knowing where the job will lead and control over their career path*		
Inspiring Future Vision *e.g., a dream or ideal they were holding on to that helped them feel energized and engaged*		

You can return to this tool again and again, using the whole thing or pulling the bits that are needed most, until you don't need it anymore because you are now an expert, coaching other leaders and developing your own unique change leadership practices. Remember, celebrate your accomplishments as you develop: these are beautiful moments!

Want More?

This book and my company, Elizabeth Moran Transformation, emerged from my belief that transformation doesn't have to be complicated. I am passionate about helping leaders, teams, and organizations navigate and evolve through constant change in the simplest way possible, leveraging their strengths and aligning their energy to realize their vision. As a consultant and executive coach, I have successfully partnered with leaders and teams, ranging in size from Fortune 500 companies to technology start-ups, as they tackle enterprise-wide change to smaller transformation projects at the business unit and team level.

Prior to starting Elizabeth Moran Transformation, I was the vice president of Global Talent & Development at ADP and have also supported successful leaders, teams, and transformations internally at Bloomberg, Lehman Brothers, Getty Images, Time Inc., and Gap Inc. In addition to my experience in technology, financial services, publishing, and retail, I have consulted with and coached leaders and teams in the professional services, pharmaceutical, energy, government, and nonprofit sectors.

I can help others be their best only if I am willing to challenge and grow myself. Relentless curiosity and the belief that deeper understanding leads to greater inner and outer freedom helps me continually reflect, question, and learn, even when it's uncomfortable. My learning journey includes a PCC-level coaching certification with the International Coaching Federation, a Strengths-Based Coaching certification from the Marcus Buckingham Company, and certification as a Neuro-Transformational Coach (practical application of neuroscience in the business context). I hold master's and doctoral degrees in clinical psychology from the California Institute of Integral Studies, using the practical application of Eastern philosophy, Western psychology, and neuroscience to create healing and greater possibility for all people.

If you'd like more help leading through your organization's current or upcoming change or additional information about Practical Change Leadership, my scalable and technology-based leadership development solution, schedule a conversation at www.elizabethmorantransformation.com

Additional Resources

I have tremendous gratitude for those teachers and authors who have helped me discover, learn, and grow, especially in finding my own voice in the transformation space. Below is a short list of books I return to again and again to expand as a coach, teacher, and human, and which were critical resources for me in writing this book. If you want to dive deeper into some of what we covered in this book, I highly recommend them.

***Helping People Change: Coaching with Compassion for Lifelong Learning and Growth*, Richard Boyatzis, Melvin Smith, and Ellen Van Oosten (Harvard Business Review Press, 2019)**
Dr. Richard Boyatzis is one of my favorite speakers and researchers, whom I had the great fortune of working with while at Lehman Brothers. I credit him for igniting the neuroscience spark in me. I love this book because he and his fellow authors use research to demonstrate that the best way to help someone change is not by mainly focusing on fixing their problems but instead helping them create and connect to a positive future vision of themselves or an inspiring dream or goal, which gives them the energy needed to change, especially when it gets tough.

***Nine Lies About Work: A Freethinking Leader's Guide to the Real World*, Marcus Buckingham and Ashley Goodall (Harvard Business Review Press, 2019)**
I got to know Marcus Buckingham and his amazing team of people while I was at ADP, and I credit them for my awakening to the power of using strengths to help me, my team, and my organization be their best. Marcus and his team were so generous in sharing their knowledge and support along the way; plus they were a ton of fun to work with! I've listed Marcus's latest

book here, but he has many others, and I recommend them all. To learn more about how you and your team or organization can leverage the power of strengths to create happier, higher-performing people, visit the Marcus Buckingham Company at www.tmbc.com.

***Resilience: The Science of Mastering Life's Greatest Challenges,* Steven M. Southwick and Dennis S. Charney (Cambridge University Press, 2012)**
This wonderful book uses research to reinforce the notion that we are all capable of becoming more resilient, no matter the context or condition. Its ten strategies are backed by research and are accessible to all.

***Becoming Supernatural: How Common People Are Doing the Uncommon,* Dr Joe Dispenza (Hay House, Inc., 2017)**
Dr. Joe Dispenza has the courage to go beyond the more traditional (and I'll say "safe") confines of science. In his groundbreaking book, he brings together the latest research from a range of fields including epigenetics, molecular biology, neurocardiology, and quantum physics to articulate a path to reach our greatest potential beyond what many of us have been taught is possible. His work found me, as these things often do, at just the right time, helping me continue my own journey of growth in a whole new way.

***Resilient: How to Grow an Unshakable Core of Calm, Strength, and Happiness,* Rick Hanson with Forrest Hanson (Harmony Books, 2018)**
What I love most about Rick Hanson's work is the simplicity and humor in his writing and speaking. In stressful times, I've applied many of his resilience-building strategies, which have helped me remain peaceful in the midst of a number of storms.

***The Technology Fallacy: How People Are the Real Key to Digital Transformation*, Gerald C. Kane, Anh Nguyen Phillips, Jonathan R. Copulsky, and Garth R. Andrus (The MIT Press, 2019)**
A friend and colleague recommended this book to me, and in the years since, I have referenced it multiple times, especially as digital transformation increases. The book is both practical and highly insightful, reminding us that at its essence, digital transformation is not about technology but about people and our ability to help them be their best during rapid technology change.

***Your Brain and Business: The Neuroscience of Great Leaders*, Srinivasan S. Pillay (Pearson Education, Inc., publishing as FT Press, 2011)**
Dr. Srini Pillay is one of my most influential teachers, encouraging me and so many others to step into and enjoy the dance between internal discomfort and possibility when we expand our hearts and minds, which is the only road to freedom. He is a courageous, humorous, and unique thinker, who helps me explore the inner realms and continue to use my authentic and unique voice to create something beautiful in the world. He has written a number of books, but I have a particular love for this one, which brings together two of my favorite topics in a practical way—neuroscience and great leadership. To learn more about Dr. Pillay, access his writing, or work with him, visit https://drsrinipillay.com and https://nbgcorporate.com

Notes

1. I Sarinopoulos et al., "Uncertainty during Anticipation Modulates Neural Responses to Aversion in Human Insula and Amygdala," *Cerebral Cortex* 20, no. 4 (April 2010): 929–940, https://academic.oup.com/cercor/article/20/4/929/306868.
2. Rick Hanson, "Take in the Good," *Rick Hanson* (website), https://www.rickhanson.net/take-in-the-good/.
3. Srinivasan S. Pillay, *Your Brain and Business: The Neuroscience of Great Leaders* (Upper Saddle River, NJ: Pearson Education, Inc., publishing as FT Press, 2011), 161.
4. Pillay, *Your Brain and Business*, 162.
5. A. I. Jack et al., "fMRI Reveals Reciprocal Inhibition between Social and Physical Cognitive Domains," *NeuroImage* 66, no. 1, (February 1, 2013): 385–401, https://www.sciencedirect.com/science/article/abs/pii/S1053811912010646?via%3Dihub; Richard Boyatzis, Melvin Smith, and Ellen Van Oosten, *Helping People Change* (Boston: Harvard Business Review Press, 2019), 85.
6. Pillay, *Your Brain and Business*, 41.
7. Tali Sharot et al., "Neural Mechanisms Mediating Optimism Bias," *Nature* 450 (November 1, 2007): 102–5, https://www.nature.com/articles/nature06280; Joe Dispenza, *Becoming Supernatural* (Carlsbad, CA: Hay House, Inc., 2017), 36-37.
8. Lang Chen et al., "Positive Attitude toward Math Supports Early Academic Success: Behavioral Evidence and Neurocognitive Mechanisms," *Psychological Science* 29, no. 3 (January 24, 2018): 379–389, https://journals.sagepub.com/doi/10.1177/0956797617735528.
9. Marcus Buckingham and Ashley Goodall, *Nine Lies about Work* (Boston: Harvard Business Review Press, 2019), 42.
10. Buckingham and Goodall, *Nine Lies about Work*, 50.
11. Pillay, *Your Brain and Business*, 46.

12. Boyatzis, Smith, and Van Oosten, *Helping People Change*, 5–6.
13. Mary Baker, "How to Reduce the Risk of Employee Change Fatigue," *Gartner* (website), October 14, 2020, https://www.gartner.com/smarterwithgartner/how-to-reduce-the-risk-of-employee-change-fatigue.
14. Buckingham and Goodall, *Nine Lies about Work*, 83.
15. Tait D. Shanafelt et al., "Career Fit and Burnout among Academic Faculty," *Archives of Internal Medicine* 169, no. 10 (May 25, 2009): 990–95, https://jamanetwork.com/journals/jamainternalmedicine/fullarticle/415000.
16. Donald E. Gibson and Ronda Roberts Callister, "Anger in Organizations: Review and Integration," *Journal of Management* 36, no. 1 (January 2010): 66–93.

Business Books

Business Books publishes practical guides and insightful non-fiction for beginners and professionals. Covering aspects from management skills, leadership and organizational change to positive work environments, career coaching and self-care for managers, our books are a valuable addition to those working in the world of business.

15 Ways to Own Your Future

Take Control of Your Destiny in Business and in Life

Michael Khouri

A 15-point blueprint for creating better collaboration, enjoyment and success in business and in life.

Paperback: 978-1-78535-300-0 ebook: 978-1-78535-301-7

The Common Excuses of the Comfortable Compromiser

Understanding Why People Oppose Your Great Idea

Matt Crossman

Comfortable compromisers block the way of anyone trying to change anything. This is your guide to their common excuses.

Paperback: 978-1-78099-595-3 ebook: 978-1-78099-596-0

Mastering the Mommy Track

Juggling Career and Kids in Uncertain Times

Erin Flynn Jay

Mastering the Mommy Track tells the stories of everyday working mothers, the challenges they have faced, and lessons learned.

Paperback: 978-1-78099-123-8 ebook: 978-1-78099-124-5

The Most Creative, Escape the Ordinary, Excel at Public Speaking Book Ever

All The Help You Will Ever Need in Giving a Speech

Philip Theibert

The 'everything you need to give an outstanding speech' book, complete with original material written by a professional speech-writer.

Paperback: 978-1-78099-672-1 ebook: 978-1-78099-673-8

Small Change, Big Deal

Money as if People Mattered

Jennifer Kavanagh

Money is about relationships: between individuals and between communities. Small is still beautiful, as peer lending model, micro-credit, shows.

Paperback: 978-1-78099-313-3 ebook: 978-1-78099-314-0

The Failing Logic of Money

Duane Mullin

Money is wasteful and cruel, causes war, crime and dysfunctional feudalism. Humankind needs happiness, peace and abundance. So banish money and use technology and knowledge to rid the world of war, crime and poverty.

Paperback: 978-1-84694-259-4 ebook: 978-1-84694-888-6

Modern Day Selling

Unlocking Your Hidden Potential

Brian Barfield

Learn how to reconnect sales associates with customers and unlock hidden sales potential.

Paperback: 978-1-78099-457-4 ebook: 978-1-78099-458-1

Readers of ebooks can buy or view any of these bestsellers by clicking on the live link in the title. Most titles are published in paperback and as an ebook. Paperbacks are available in traditional bookshops. Both print and ebook formats are available online.

Find more titles and sign up to our readers' newsletter at http://www.jhpbusiness-books.com/

Facebook: https://www.facebook.com/JHPNonFiction/

Twitter: @JHPNonFiction